Stuff We Had in the '50s and '60s

Pam Van Der Kooy

Published by:
Boolarong Press
38/1631 Wynnum Road
Tingalpa Qld 4173
Australia.
www.boolarongpress.com.au

First published 2019

A catalogue record for this book is available from the National Library of Australia

ISBN: 9781925877366 (paperback)

Typeset by Boolarong Press in Spectral 12pt

Edited by Wordwright, www.wordwrightediting.com.au.

Cover design by Boolarong Press

Printed and bound by Watson Ferguson & Company, Tingalpa, Australia

Contents

Baby boomer (beɪbi buːmər): noun

Australia's Baby Boomers were born between 1946 and 1966 during the post-war economic boom.

Australian Bureau of Statistics

Almost exactly nine months after WWII ended, "the cry of the baby was heard across the land ..."

Landon Jones
Historian

My earliest memory is from when I must have been around two, sitting on the floor of our hallway. I had a cold and had been miserable all day. Dad had come home from work and as I turned myself around in a circle, I found a small, sparkly purse that he had placed on the floor for me to find.

What was your first memory?

Herein lies the purpose of this book.

It is an incomplete collection of *stuff* from the 1950s and 1960s with facts, history, anecdotes and memories to be used as catalysts for your own memories of that time — good or bad, golden or otherwise.

When my father's book *Aniseed Balls, Billy Carts and Clotheslines: An ABC to Growing up in the Thirties* was published, one of the most frequent comments we had was that people were going to use it to give to their kids and grandies to show them what life was like. How much better would it be to have space to add your own memories?

Introducing the "Some of my own stuff" pages.

Fill them up with YOUR stuff.

Mum and Dad purchased their second house in Mt Gravatt in 1957, moving from Enoggera to be closer to Upper Mt Gravatt State School where Dad was teaching. The house backed on to the Mt Gravatt reserve, a key decision in their purchase as dad was a keen naturalist and loved all things to do with the bush. The backyard, under Dad's and Mum's nurturing, became a mini rainforest with staghorns that wrapped their green arms around the native trees, lichen-encrusted rocks that edged wild gardens, and a wooden bridge that spanned a natural waterway (in wet weather anyway) that ran through our backyard. There was a native bee log, camping area and fireplace, and a large ground level birdbath.

I had a charmed childhood.

Stuff we had in the lounge room

When Mum and Dad married in 1952, they purchased a lounge suite from Diamonds at Newmarket. It was an overstuffed, maroon velvety thing with incised swirls and wooden armrests that weren't any good for lounging on to watch TV (not really a consideration at the time of purchase). The curtains were dark green velvet with a lighter sheer drape underneath. Later they invested in some aluminum-bladed venetian blinds for the bedrooms. These were the wide blades and just as annoying to clean as they are now.

Our black, amazingly heavy, Bakelite phone lived in the lounge room. I think most people's phones were there and it wasn't until space-age things like wall phones came in that anyone thought to place them anywhere else. We had a six-digit phone number (492368), but I remember when we used to go to Coolum for our holidays, the caravan park had only one number for its phone number, which I found quite amazing.

A very big feature in our lounge room, and indeed part of the fabric of our home, was the Victor upright piano. This old treasure had been Mum's since she was very young and had been hauled up the Blackall Range in 1934 on the back of my Grandpa's truck. Mum was (and still is at the time of publication, at the age of 93) an extremely talented pianist, and during the late 1940s and early 1950s, played for ABC radio 4QR live performance relays from their Brisbane studios. She even released a CD when she was 87. Unfortunately, the gene pool was a bit diluted by the time it got to me.

The Box Brownie camera was still an incredibly popular item for families. Originally marketed in 1900 for just $1 by Kodak Eastman, particularly to increase sales of the roll film just invented, it put cameras into the hands of the general population. A simple cardboard box about 13 cm tall and covered in fake leather, it had a small round opening at the front and operated as a simple point and shoot camera. Kodak continued to produce cameras with the Brownie tag until the 1980s, but they had gone far beyond the original box version.

Early in the 1960s, Kodak launched its sensational Instamatic with the new easy-to-load, self-contained 126 film cartridge, 'making it easy for children and women alike to take photos' (bless them). They were easy to use and encouraged people to take many photos with their 12 or 20 exposure films (and pay for lots of prints). Kodak and other companies continued to develop this range of cameras for many years to come, incorporating flashcubes and manual add-ons.

SLR cameras that could turn film into slides really came into their own during the 1950s and 1960s, with Kodak and Agfa vying for 35 mm film popularity. I could always tell when Dad had used Agfa film, as it seemed to have more of a bluish tinge. Dad had a Voigtlander camera and leather case, with a petal style flash.

It was always exciting when Dad sent away the finished film and we waited for the yellow-lidded box to arrive with each slide mounted in its cardboard (and later, plastic) frame.

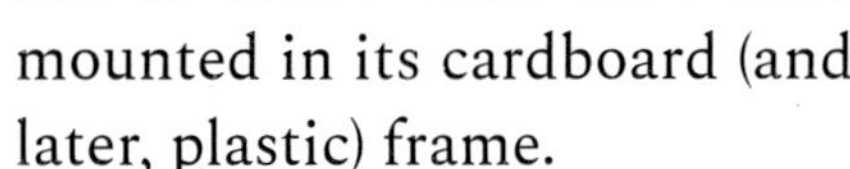

Dad would check each slide with the viewer and then the projector was plugged in, the screen hauled up and we sat and watched our holiday shots in full colour. Slide nights were the thing for a while, and you got to know which invitations were probably best to politely decline to avoid having to poke your eyes out with knitting needles as you watched the 20th slide of Pauly and Susan at the beach.

Dad, bless him, religiously coded each slide, and wrote them up in a book with date, place and names. This made my life so much easier when I finally stopped procrastinating and scanned all several hundred of them into digital format.

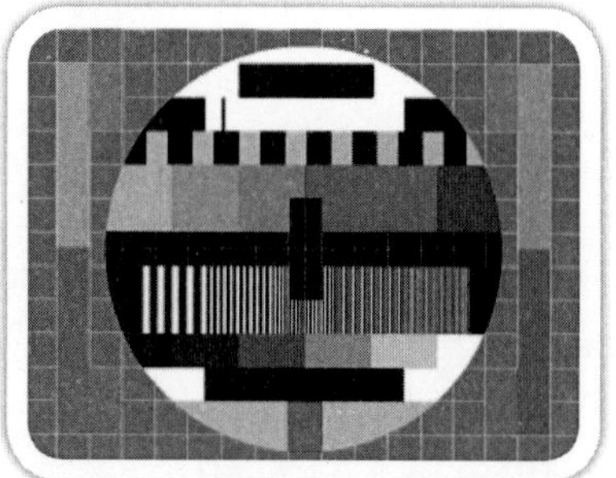

Although television began in Australia in 1956, it would be a couple of years before Brisbane came online, with QTQ (Channel 9) being the first to broadcast in August 1959 and BTQ 7 and ABQ 2 starting in November. TVQ 0 didn't start until 1965. Of course, stations didn't broadcast all day, often not starting until the afternoon, and stopping again before midnight each night. Each had their own closing program, often incorporating the national anthem, test pattern and epilogue, while TVQ 0 had the thought-provoking *Just A Minute.*

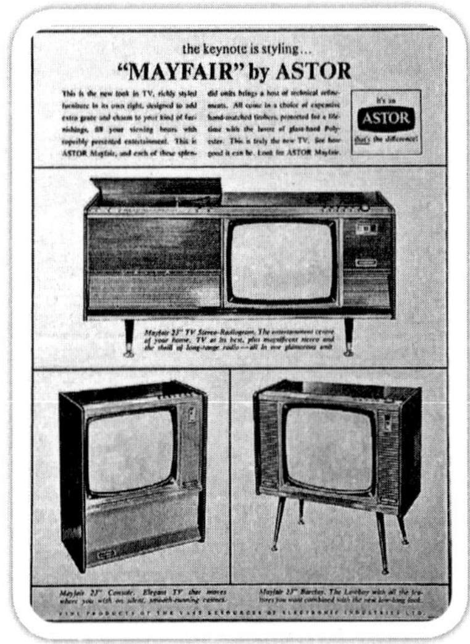

TV sets were an item of furniture in their own right, taking pride of place in the lounge room with all the lounge chairs arranged to take full viewing advantage. The screens were set into a wooden surround with speakers and dials and knobs. Some were so big you had no option but to arrange the lounge room around them.

Television was an expense that many families couldn't afford so they would still listen to the radio, tuning in to *Blue Hills*, or the kids (if they weren't outside playing) enjoying *Children's Hour* or *Kindergarten of the Air.* There was *Amateur Hour*, *Dad and Dave*, *Biggles*, *Tarzan*, *Hop Harrigan*, *Davy Crockett*, *The Goon Show* and Bob Dyer's game shows.

Although many of the big valve radios still took pride of place in the lounge rooms, many households were moving on to the more portable valve radios, and then to the even more convenient transistor radios. We had a valve radio in the kitchen on the shelf — a brown thing with the station finder that you could wind along. You would have to turn it on and let it warm up a bit before it started to work.

The first transistor radios were still reasonably heavy, but they gradually became smaller, cheaper and perfect to take with you from room to room or outside. They first appeared in Australia in 1954 and became an enormous success during the 1960s, freeing up the younger generation to listen to their own music in their own space. When we upgraded to a transistor radio, it too lived in the kitchen, but also accompanied us on our trips in the caravan, where I would listen avidly to *Kindergarten of the Air*.

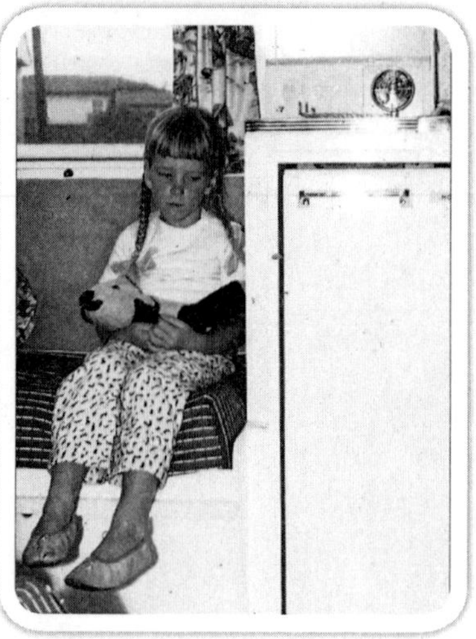

If you owned a television, you had to pay the government for a Television Viewing Licence for the pleasure of viewing. It cost 5 pounds and this was on top of the existing radio licence (Broadcast Listener's Licence) of 2 pounds 15 shillings. If you didn't pay, you ran the risk of a fine of up to 50 pounds. Some people hid the antennae in the roof cavity or their TVs in cupboards in case the door-to-door checks came knocking. Our first television was rented. I think Dad was hoping it might just be a fad that would fade away. Nuh.

TV Week (or as it was then, *TV Radio Week*) started in Melbourne in 1957 and gradually moved into the other states as TV came online. Television had an enormous impact on day-to-day life in households, with manufacturers catering for the change in habits with TV trays, TV meals and folding TV tables, not to mention the switch to couch potato status.

It influenced children's activities and outside time and, if they sat too close, gave them square eyes. It was the curse for parents who thought their children should be studying and not wasting their time in front of the box. My friend's father used to take the tubes out of the TV when her sister had exams, not realising that her older brother knew how to get into the toolbox where the tubes were hidden and put them back in. They just had to make sure the TV was cool by the time Dad got home from work.

Classic TV of the time were shows like *The Cottee's Happy Hour*, *Roy Rogers*, *Annie Oakley*, *Rawhide*, *Wagon Train*, *Bilko*, *The Samurai*, *Mr Squiggle*, *Andy Pandy*, *Astro Boy*, *Bill & Ben*, *Jill & Beanpole*, *Adventure Island*, *Magic Roundabout* (with Dougal the dog),

Romper Room, *Play School*, *Here's Humphrey*, *Magic Circle Club*, *Diver Dan*, *The Jetsons*, *Mister Ed*, *The Cisco Kid* ("Hey Cisco", "Hey Pancho"), *Captain Pugwash*, *Lippy the Lion and Hardy Har Har* ("Exit stage left"), *Sooty*, *Daktari* (with Clarence the cross-eyed lion), *Looney Tunes*, *Merrie Melodies*, *Road Runner* and others, *Casper*, *F Troop*, *Thunderbirds*, *My Favourite Martian*, *Skippy*, *Gilligan's Island*, *The Beverley Hillbillies*, *Bewitched*, *I Dream of Jeannie*, *The Lone Ranger* ("Hi-ho Silver, away..."), *Lassie*, *Rin Tin Tin*, *The Munsters*, *The Addams Family*, *Petticoat Junction*, *Zorro*, *The Andy Griffith Show*, *Gomer Pyle*, *Hogan's Heroes*, *Batman*, *The Flintstones*, *The Ghost and Mrs Muir*, *Candid Camera* with Alan Fudd ("When you least expect it, you're elected, you're the star today ... smile, you're on Candid Camera"), Disney on Sunday night, and the *TAA Junior Flyers Club* or the *Channel Niners* with Jim Iliffe. Some of these shows were made into annual books to capitalise on the merchandising. Ready Mr Music ...

Romper bomper stomper boo
Tell me tell me tell me do
Magic mirror please tell me today
Did all my friends have fun at play?

She wouldn't know if I did — she never saw me ... cow.

Professor Julius Sumner Miller, with his crazy hair and dramatic teaching methods, asked, "Why is it so?" on his science program on the ABC and made science exciting. From 1962 to 1986, he made 27 visits to Australia to give lectures and demonstrations at The University of Sydney. These lectures were televised for many years.

Sunday night was Disney night and I remember vividly, in 1966, after seeing in the newspaper that Walt Disney had died, being so devastated — not because of the loss of such a great mind but because I thought my Sunday night's Disney show was finished.

Aside from the news (which we found quite boring) and the weather (with the little weathervane rooster that turned around), Mum and Dad didn't watch very much TV. If they did, it was usually after I went to bed, so I didn't really know what their favourites were. Adult-oriented shows included *Four Corners*, *Sea Hunt*, *Dragnet*, *Beauty and the Beast*, *Maverick*, *Homicide*, *Bellbird*, *Today Tonight*, *The Mavis Bramston Show*, *Riptide*, *Division 4*, *Bandstand*, *6 O'Clock Rock*, *Laugh-in*, *The Dick van Dyke Show*, *Bonanza*, *The Phyllis Diller Show*, *Star Trek*, *Doctor Who* and Bob Dyer's *Pick a Box*.

Right up until the 1960s, you would rarely, if ever, see a couple in a movie or television shown in bed together. They were always depicted as sleeping in separate twin beds, usually with a bedside table in between so they couldn't even push the beds together when you weren't watching. Darrin and Samantha Stephens on *Bewitched* were actually the first TV couple who were allowed in the same bed.

Encyclopaedia Britannica and *Funk & Wagnell* vied for space on the bookshelf. We never had a set of them, but we did have a set of Waverley's that belonged to my Mum, featuring Queen Elizabeth as a toddler. They were fine if you wanted to find out about Magellan or Christopher Columbus, but pretty woeful in the space race department. There was also a *Pears Cyclopaedia* that was so useful when we had to find synonyms or antonyms for homework, as it had a whole section on it. Sold from door to door, the *Encyclopaedia Britannica* was a 20-plus volume investment, sometimes paid for in instalments, such was the outlay.

Dad was a pipe smoker and would have his ritual after dinner of filling his pipe with tobacco from the Log Cabin or Erinmore tin and lighting up. That was the only time he smoked during the day and it would only be one pipe. Very rarely would he lash out and buy cigarettes. They would usually be a gift of a box of Benson and Hedges.

He had a very trendy black glass (onyx) and chrome smoker's stand complete with matchbox holder and ashtray. He also had a couple of ashtrays that were glass, with a replica Goodrich car tyre inside. We used to like to pull the tyres off the ashtray and roll them down the hallway. Other people had those really cool ash trays that had a knob on the top that, when you pushed them, the bottom would spin the ash away to the bottom tray.

Bryant and May, or Brymay (originally a UK company), were the first red-headed safety match producers in Australia with a factory in Richmond Victoria from 1909, but it wasn't until 1946 that the well-known Redhead logo was first used. The hairdo on the logo changed in 1958 to reflect changing fashions. They were called "safety matches" as previous matches were made using poisonous white phosphorous and called "strike anywhere" matches, as you could light them up on almost any surface. Naturally, they were something of a fire hazard (aside from the fact that the poisonous phosphorous produced horrendous disfigurement in the workers called "phossy jaw"). The safety match could only be struck on the prepared side of the box that had been coated with non-poisonous or amorphous phosphorous. Brymay is now owned by Swedish Match and they are manufactured overseas.

Federal was the other major brand of matches in Australia and hailed from New South Wales. They seemed to have kept to their territory for a while at least. Matchboxes were in demand for making small items of furniture for doll's houses or for insect collectors to keep their dead bugs in.

Hanna Group began in 1957 and is responsible for many of the advertising matchbooks you pick up at hotels and clubs.

Before Gillette developed the Cricket disposable lighter in 1972, and Bic launched theirs in 1973, lighters ranged from utilitarian to expensive fashion pieces. Dad had a couple. Both were lift-arm, petrol and flint lighters. One was an Estralite and the other a Polo. Now and then the flint would need replacing with Auermetall (cereisen) flints. Ronson, Dunhill and Zippo were also popular brands at the time.

The radiogram, as with the early TV, was also a piece of furniture, being in part a

sideboard, some with a lift up lid and others with a fold down door. It contained both the radio and record player. We didn't have one, but Dad invested in a reel-to-reel tape player that had two-track capability. You had to be so careful on which track you were recording so you didn't wipe out The Mikado from the other track.

He later purchased Marantz sound systems that, by then, were separate units that you could fit into your existing furnishings and decor. They had the capacity to stack a few records to play one after another and we thought we were made.

Records weren't just for adults — we kids had our storybook records as well. I loved my *Heidi* storybook, an "original little long play recording" with a bell sound to know when to turn the page.

The older sister of one of my friends, who was extremely cool, hip and groovy, had a portable record player in a flash red suitcase, along with a suitably impressive collection of 45s. I'm sure the youngster had one in the annexe next to ours at Pialba in 1967 when we were regaled with Nancy Sinatra singing "These Boots are Made for Walkin'" — over and over and over and over and over again. Obviously it was a powered site.

My friends were lucky enough to have an original lava lamp. Many hours were spent in front of it just watching the goop rise to the surface and blob back down again. It was invented in 1963 in the UK by a Mr Craven-Walker and was originally called the Astro lava lamp. They were THE art piece of the swinging 60s and have had a bit of a revival lately.

I love seeing things coming back and the younger ones thinking their generation is so clever "inventing" them. A bit like ... "How do you know the words to that song Mum?" You know what I mean?

Being brought up as good Methodists, it was always secret business to show our friends the bottle of Yalumba Hospital Brandy that was hidden in the depths of our sideboard. It went down by about three tablespoons a year when Mum made Christmas cake.

Dad's morning ritual would be to get up and retrieve *The Courier-Mail* from the front yard that was rolled up and held with a narrow piece of brown paper wrapped around it. He would sit at the table with a nice cup of tea while Mum got breakfast ready. We would get to read the cartoons of

Blondie and Dagwood, Ginger Meggs, Dick Tracy or The Phantom.

Women's magazines provided a small escape now and then for mums with the *Australian Women's Weekly* (which was a weekly then), *Australian Home Journal*, *New Idea*, *Home Beautiful* and *Woman's Day*. They had clothes patterns, decorating ideas, gossip and recipes, some of which are probably best left in the past.

Women's magazines had their very own domestic goddesses who reigned supreme like Margeurite Patten and Margaret Fulton (many kitchens had her classic 1968 release *The Margaret Fulton Cookbook*), who provided recipes and helpful home hints.

Readers Digest, full of light reading and favourite subjects, had been available in Australia since 1946 and was in most doctors' and dentists' waiting rooms, while the *National Geographic* magazine, with its distinctive yellow border, provided food for the enquiring mind (and small boys who liked to look for photos of native women).

In 1959, *National Geographic* had its first photographic front cover, still with the yellow border.

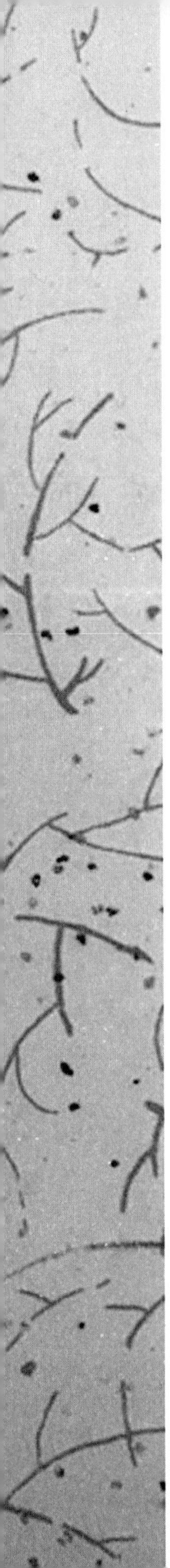

Stuff we had in the kitchen

Where previously kitchens had been relegated to the back of the house, the 1950s kitchen was designed to be the centre of the family home. This was due in part to the modernisation and development of many timesaving appliances, making it a much more user-friendly, pleasant place for everyone to be.

Kitchens in the 1950s had their own style, with cupboards (wall and floor) often having rounded ends with open shelves. In fact, the wall cupboards were often angled up and out a bit with glass sliding doors.

As the walls in our house were fibrous plaster, meaning they had a fibre (like coconut fibre) mixed into the plaster, the walls were a little uneven, so wallpaper was

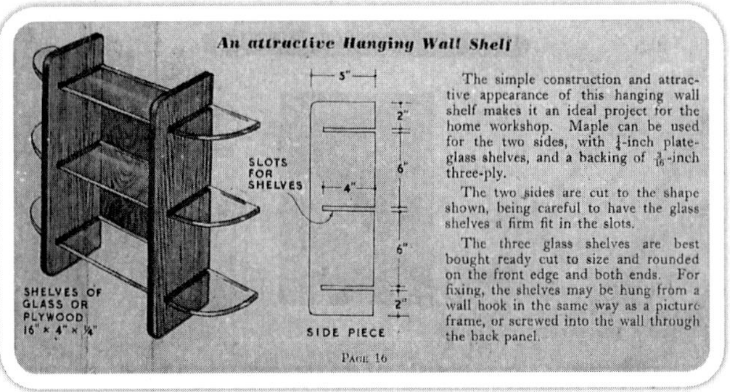

An attractive Hanging Wall Shelf

The simple construction and attractive appearance of this hanging wall shelf makes it an ideal project for the home workshop. Maple can be used for the two sides, with $\frac{1}{4}$-inch plate-glass shelves, and a backing of $\frac{3}{16}$-inch three-ply.

The two sides are cut to the shape shown, being careful to have the glass shelves a firm fit in the slots.

The three glass shelves are best bought ready cut to size and rounded on the front edge and both ends. For fixing, the shelves may be hung from a wall hook in the same way as a picture frame, or screwed into the wall through the back panel.

PAGE 16

Image from *The Solvol Handy Home Book*

used as a decorative cover-up, even in the kitchen.

The ceilings were also made with fibrous plaster and then given a coat of quick drying calcimine paint (bit like the whitewash of old during spring cleaning to freshen up the place), a calcium carbonate product which was all well and good and, when painted with ceiling paint, looked lovely. Unfortunately, after a while the painted finish on top would eventually fail and start to peel away, a common scenario in houses of that time. Dad grew tired of fixing the problem so installed polystyrene squares over the kitchen ceiling. There were the decorative cornices and, if you were really flash, you had a plaster rose around the light fixture.

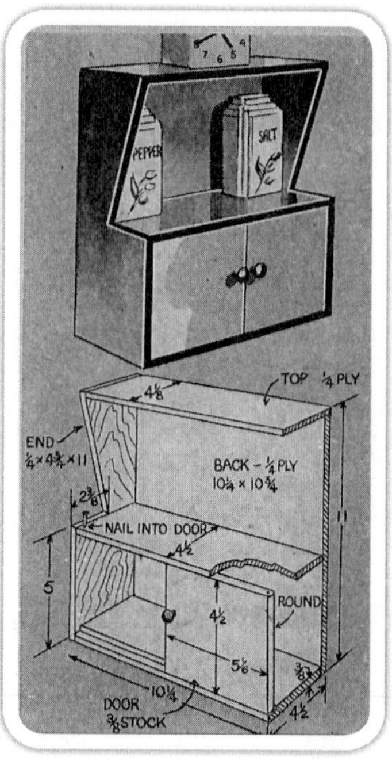

Image from *The Solvol Handy Home Book*

Laminex manufactured and distributed plastic laminates in Australia from 1934, beginning its range of interior décor product in the late 1940s. Moving in 1952 to larger premises, the company was able to expand its product range, and the early 1950s saw the range of colours and patterns increase.

Formica, another high-pressure laminate, began importing to Australia in 1947, with colours and patterns including their famous *Skylark*. Timber look laminates appeared in 1960 and became one of their best sellers, with the company starting manufacturing at Thornleigh in the same year.

The colour range from the 1940s, with its Coral Pink and Apple Green, was still part of the palette in the early 1950s (as our bathroom would show), but progressed to stronger colours and then patterns like marble, timber grain, weaves and metallic thread. We had Laminex on our kitchen table with threads and bits of "glitter".

This introduced a versatile product for the modern kitchen that was hygienic, practical and attractive, bringing both colour and design to what was previously a less considered area of the house as far as décor went. Due to its plastic content, many housewives found out the hard way that their new bench tops didn't mix well with hot saucepan bases. Laminex and chrome were teamed together on the Namco chairs and tables, and the chrome formed edging around laminated bench tops.

To add to the mix of colour and pattern, Fablon and Con-Tact entered the market.

The self-adhesive plastic sheeting was used to cover shelves, tables, cupboards, trays — basically anything that wasn't moving. It even entered the homemade jewellery market with small strips wrapped around paperclips and linked together to make a very funky necklace for gran.

Designs on Laminex, Fablon, Con-tact and fabric of the time was heavily influenced first by the happenings in the field of atomic science from the 1940s, which then morphed into the space race, with starbursts, constellations and molecules.

We have an Australian to thank for the invention of refrigeration. In 1854, James Harrison developed a means of creating ice that allowed refrigerated meat to be shipped to Britain, arriving in a wholesome, edible state. The electric refrigerator, or fridge as we love to call it, took another hundred years to be developed into a domestic mainstay in the Australian household, with 77 per cent of Brisbane households owning one by 1955. That number had jumped to 94 per cent by 1964.

Before the electric, gas or even kerosene versions, the icebox was the way of keeping things relatively cool. Each week, the iceman would arrive carrying a block of ice, with the big calipers placing it in the top section. There was a drip tray to catch the water as the block melted, and it was important to make sure the tray was emptied regularly to avoid a puddle on the floor. Opening the door was kept to a minimum ... none of this standing around peering at the contents of the fridge deciding what to eat or drink.

When Mum and Dad were first married, they had an electric-powered Hallstrom Silent Knight refrigerator, which was developed in the mid-1930s and became very popular as it was a much cheaper option than imported refrigerators, although it was quite expensive to run. Hallstrom's factory was in Willoughby, New South Wales, and during the war it produced munitions as well as refrigerators.

Moving to their new home in Mt Gravatt in 1957, they purchased a GE upright which came with a small freezer section. This was accessed from the main part of the fridge, and, especially in humid weather, would ice up to glacial levels if left unchecked, requiring defrosting. This could be a major operation, with warnings from Dad not to use metal implements in case we punctured the pipework.

We had a blue and white Canned Cold Magic Brick tin in the freezer which took up a fair bit of the space, but was super useful in our metal esky. Another popular version of the cold brick was in a tartan-patterned tin. In summer, there was always a supply of homemade cordial ice blocks in their cylindrical moulds, while a ready supply of ice cubes was now possible using the aluminium ice tray with the lever. This had been developed by American Edward Roberts, a design engineer with GE in the early 1950s.

The latch system on the doors of the early refrigerators meant they could only be opened from the outside. This led to the tragic suffocation deaths of some children who thought they might hide in the fridge or play in one that had been dumped. Dad monstered (in the best possible way) our fridge and changed it so there was no longer a problem. Today, fridges are manufactured to close with magnets. Our GE fridge from the mid 1950s is still powering along when we need it, although it has had a dark blue spray paint to match teenager's tastes. The electricity meter dial spins a bit faster whenever it is on.

We got to make our own ice cream from Carnation Milk and, before we had a MixMaster, whipping it up was done with a hand rotary beater. It was a family affair and we all took turns beating it up until our arms ached, begging for a spoonful. To make it creamier, it had to come out after being partly frozen and whipped again. It was all so worth it!

The electric frypan, so much a part of everyone's household these days, was invented in the US in 1953. Sunbeam released their model in Australia in 1955 along with their pop-up toaster — a welcome revolution in toasting, spurred on by the increase in popularity of sliced bread. Many's the slice of bread that was burnt beyond recognition in our old side opening toaster ... the only good thing about there not being smoke alarms at that time.

Ken Wood from Britain launched the Kenwood Chef (so that's where the name came from) in 1950. It was basically a complete redesign of the Sunbeam Mixmaster, but had several other functions added to it. In 1960, it was redesigned by Kenneth Grange into what is the familiar shape of today, and it was a big day when we purchased ours (second-hand).

A multitude of cakes, biscuits, pavlovas, desserts and milk shakes were prepared with this machine using the blender and its other attachments — and it's still going strong. The best thing about the Kenwood was that the K shaped beater was easy to get your tongue around, so bits of chocolate cake batter were never missed. The whisk was a different matter with its multiple wires — tricky to say the least, but we managed.

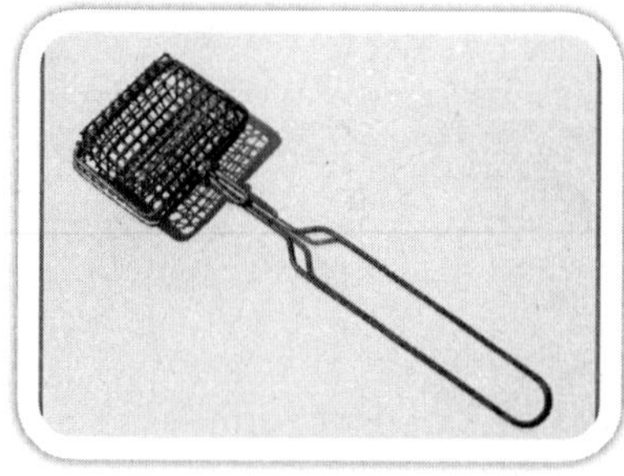

Washing up liquid wasn't in our cupboard when I was a small thing. There was the wire soap saver with its cake of Sunlight Soap that would get swooshed around in the hot water to get some suds happening. Later, Madge the manicurist (Robina Beard) was to convince us that Palmolive dishwashing detergent was "mild on hands while you do the dishes ... you're soaking in it!!" And so Palmolive became a trusted brand. The mop-headed, wire-handled dish cleaner was used to clean the plates and then, without rinsing (ewwww), they were put on the draining tray. Drying up was part and parcel of family life and I guess the towel removed a fair amount of toxic leftovers and debris. Double sinks were just not a thing. Our single stainless steel sink had drain boards on either side, a stainless steel splash back and an interesting rod-like gallery that ran around the back of the sink. Not sure what it was for.

The first Tupperware party was held in Melbourne in 1961. Mums around the country just knew they would love Tupperware because of its "famous seal that guarded foods and flavours, it was leak proof and stacked in any position, you could freeze it and save time and money and it was durable yet feather-light" — at least that was what the ads said. It was expensive BUT it had a lifetime guarantee — and I still have some of Mum's Tupperware from when I was a kid.

Earl Silas Tupper invented Tupperware in the USA in 1946 and tried selling it through hardware and department stores. It didn't take off until the party plan concept came along. With sales in 2017 of over US$2 billion, it seems they took the right sales tactic. Tupperware changed its colours and designs to match whatever was *de rigueur* at the time. From the translucent pastels of the early 1960s, it transformed into the solid oranges, green, yellows and browns of the late 1960s. It seemed every house had some Tupperware.

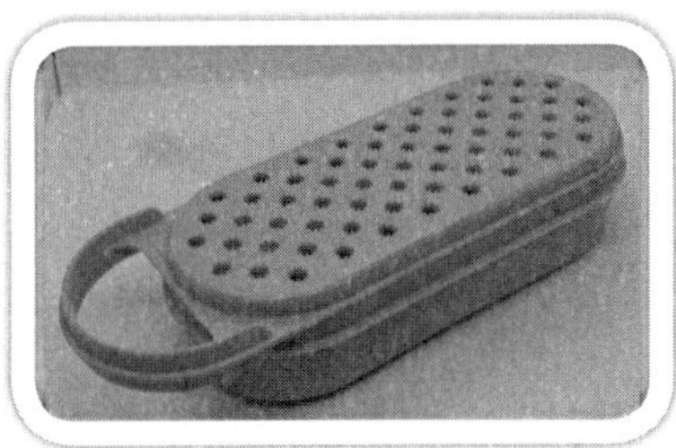

With our love of all things plastic taking off, we welcomed Glad Wrap into the kitchen. You could cover a bowl of salad, flick it with your finger and then turn it upside down and nothing would fall out.

In 1966, Glad Wrap was the first plastic cling wrap introduced into Australia. It was developed by research chemist Douglas Ford, and was originally marketed in the USA as a competitor for Saran wrap, with the promise of a safer plastic being made from polyethylene as opposed to Saran's polyvinylidene chloride — even sounds nasty!

Lady Casey, the wife of Governor-General Richard Casey, entered a *Women's Weekly* competition (and surprisingly won) about the best use for Glad Wrap. Her winning response suggested that "one could cover the hors d'oeuvres at your garden party before the guests arrive". What a coup for Glad Wrap to have such a prominent figure endorse their product! The second prizewinner, from Western Sydney, suggested using it to wrap up buttons that were the same to keep them sorted.

Of course, prior to Glad Wrap, foods were covered with a plate or wrapped in paper or waxed greaseproof paper (which is really hard to get nowadays). Mum made her own plastic covers for bowls out of a circle of plastic and stitched elastic around the edge, bit like a shower cap.

We wrapped our rubbish each night in newspaper and put it in the bin outside. The 55-litre bin was galvanised and always seemed big enough for what we needed to get rid of. Early in the morning, tucked up in bed, we would hear the garbo crunching up our gravel driveway to pick up the bin, run it back to the truck and empty it, then run back up the drive and replace it. They must have been incredibly strong and fit. We also had a large round paper bin that was collected every couple of months by APM (Australian Paper Mills).

Mum was the queen of bottled fruit and would always have a supply of peaches and pears for dessert that had been bottled in her green, stove-top Vacola bottling pan. Dad even built a special cupboard in which to store her bottled fruit.

Joseph Fowler, nephew of George Fowler who had set up a preserving company in the UK, moved to Australia in 1915 and set up his own company (later called Fowler's Vacola) using a unique vacuum preserving method that relied on the content's acidity and heating to sterilise and seal jars using rubber rings, metal lids and clips. The jars were placed in a pan of water that would be heated with a thermometer used to ensure the correct temperature of 92 degrees was reached over an hour, allowing air to escape from the lids, thus creating a vacuum as it cooled.

The pressure cooker was another kitchen staple with its locked-on lid and little pressure valve singing on the top. Of course, there are lots of horror stories associated with it, but we had endless supplies of steak and kidney along with stews, chops that melted off the bone, and bacon bone soup (sorry Mum, but I detested it and the pervading smell!).

Mum would buy meat, cut it in strips and then feed it into the manual mincer that was attached to the table. Chris was always warned to stand back in case his fingers got caught. She had given it away by the time I came along.

Flour sifters had a handle to turn manually, eventually changing into the spring-loaded handle.

Before Wiltshire introduced their Staysharp series in 1969, knife sharpeners were in the cutlery drawer, or a steel from the carving set was used. Occasionally, a door-to-door knife and scissor sharpening man would come around, take your implements and hone them to a razor sharpness. I can't imagine handing them over these days. Dad had a whetstone in the shed and would take mum's knives up there to sharpen them.

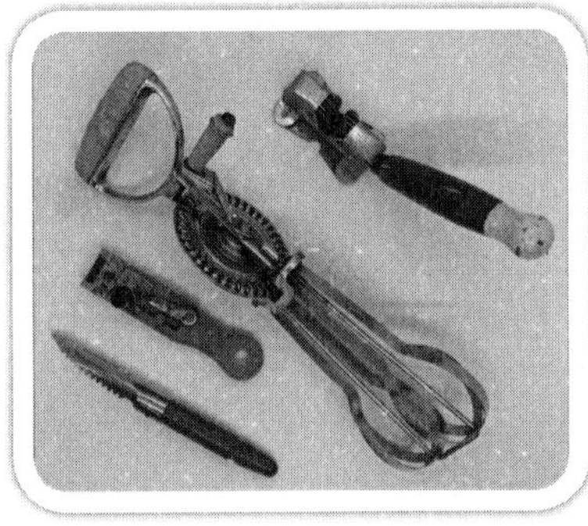

Our electric Crown stove and oven were a pretty flash, elevated, side-by-side combo model, with cupboards underneath that meant you didn't have to bend down to use the oven. It was heavy-duty enamel with the thermometer gauge on the front of the oven door. The stove elements were solid, and the solid oven door (no glass window to watch the cakes rising) closed by lifting it up and over a hook.

Crown stoves were manufactured locally in Greenslopes and Woolloongabba by The Crown Stove and Foundry Company. Started in 1912 by Mr Carl Knoblauth, they originally made wood fuel and gas stoves, heaters and boilers. Their foray into the electric market began in 1931. Interestingly, if you look at the logo for Crown, check out the font on the capital C — look familiar??

Anodised aluminium, both plain and in all of its gloriously shiny colours, pervaded the kitchen scene with cups, teasets, canisters, milkshake cups, saucepans, myriad baking items and even knitting needles. Who can forget the neat little set of picnic cups in their zip up vinyl case?

Bakelite, named for the Belgian-American chemist who invented it in 1907, Baekeland, (I just have to add the chemical name for it ... polyoxybenzylmethylenglycolanhydride) was the first plastic made using synthetic components. There were still a number of items made from Bakelite that most homes of the 1950s had, including the classic black telephone. By that time, it also came in a range of colours from translucent to marbled shades, and was even part of the fashion and jewellery industry. Plastic started to edge Bakelite out in the manufacture of everyday items, although Bakelite still held its place in the electrical field due to its great insulating properties.

Kitchens had to have canisters for just about everything and they were all named ... even if you didn't use much rice you still had a rice canister. Gay Plastics and Gay Ware were made in Australia by Pierwood Plastics from around 1950 through to 1956, when Nylex took over the patterns. They made the classic canisters with the raised initial letter of the contents, as well as myriad other kitchen essentials, including honey pots, salt and pepper shakers, cake keepers and tea dispensers.

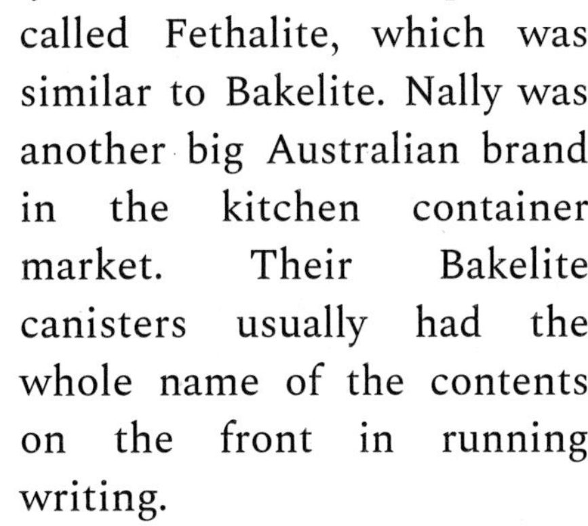

It seems they were made from a product called Fethalite, which was similar to Bakelite. Nally was another big Australian brand in the kitchen container market. Their Bakelite canisters usually had the whole name of the contents on the front in running writing.

No self-respecting hostess of the day would be without the punch bowl with the little cups hanging off hooks around the edge. The big bowl would sit on an inverted bowl to give it extra height. Also, on the patio table on those hot summer days, would be the glass jug and glasses set, a frequent wedding present back in the 1950s (like the salad spinner in the 1990s). Another wedding present of the time was the set of teacups that had different colours inside the cup to the outside, to the saucer. Mum had a set of these that she kept in our angled kitchen wall cupboard.

As kids we would often make a milkshake at my friend Julie's place and, joy oh joy, in her glass doored hutch, she had a straw dispenser with real paper straws. It was just like being at the milk bar. Many years later when she cleaned out her Mum's house, she passed it on to me.

Every year, Mum would pull everything out of the cupboards in the kitchen, wrap a hanky around her face, and spray them with a hand pump atomiser sprayer using Checkpest, a noxious concoction that was probably DDT or Dieldrin. She eventually gave over to a professional pest man who would deposit a toxic gel on the inside of the cupboard doors that seemed to do the trick.

This may have coincided with the release of *Silent Spring* by Rachel Carson in the early 1960s, and concerns over the environmental and health impacts of these and other equally toxic chemicals that were in most people's back shed.

> *If we are going to live so intimately with these chemicals — eating and drinking them, taking them into the very marrow of our bones — we had better know something about their nature and their power.* Rachel Carson, *Silent Spring* 1962

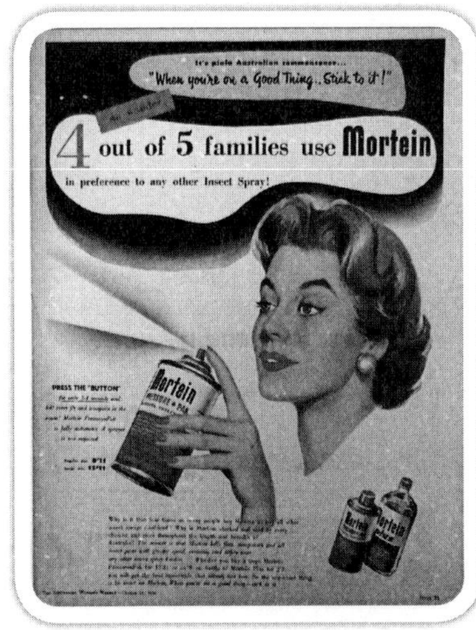

Well known Mortein goes way back to the 1870s when a German immigrant produced a pyrethrum extract to ward off insects. The story goes that Mortein is a combination of the French word for dead (mort) and the German word for one (ein). Originally a powder that was sprinkled, a squeezy puffer came about in the 1920s followed by a liquid version. Mixing it up with kerosene, a pump pack sprayed it onto the insects — a Eureka moment in pest control history. Pressure packs took over in the 1950s from the pump pack, and Louie the Fly hit the TV in 1957. By the 1960s, every child could sing the Louie the Fly song word for word. Awesome publicity!

Louie the Fly, I'm Louie the Fly,

Straight from rubbish tip to you.

Spreading disease with the greatest of ease,

Straight from rubbish tip to you.

I'm bad and mean and mighty unclean.

Afraid of no-one, 'cept the man with the can of Mortein,

Hate that word Mortein.

One spray and Louie the Fly,

Apple of his old mother's eye was dead,

Poor dead Louie, Louie the Fly, a victim of Mortein.

Mortein.

And remember ... "when you're on a good thing, stick to it!"

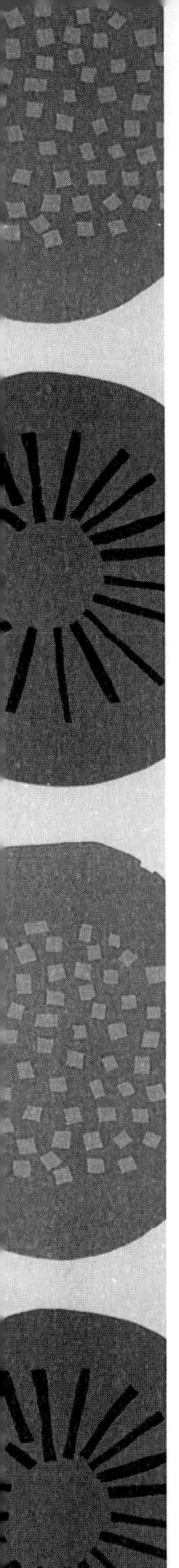

Stuff we had to eat and drink

Breakfast was usually a hot meal for our family and Mum would whip up bacon and eggs before we went to school. Healthy ideals hit in the 1960s along with Dr Vogel's grainy bread (which we weren't too fond of) and foreign chook food called muesli. Needless to say, my brother and I weren't terribly impressed and angled for cereals if we had to make the change from a hot breakfast. Of course, porridge was the go in winter, lavished with golden syrup from the spring-loaded pouring jar or brown sugar. We occasionally had Cerevite, a semolina wheat porridge that I think was shamelessly promoted (or something similar was) on

Romper Room while the children were drinking their milk.

For quite a while Kellogg's Cornflakes were the mainstay until they were surpassed in our family by Skippy cornflakes which, apparently, were the "eatingest cornflakes ever made".

Cereal packets often had a small toy inside. There were collections of trains, small horses, dogs, international costumes, planes and other items that inspired us to eat big bowlsful just so we could open the next packet. The toys were in with the cornflakes in a waxed packet so we had to dig down deep to extract them — usually while Mum wasn't watching our less than sterile hands going in. Other cereals had the little toys to assemble in a plastic packet, the pieces all linked together onto a plastic rim. Mum used to save these up for us for the holidays.

Special treat cereals we had on the holidays were the Kellogg's variety packs (great for camping but never enough of the REALLY nice ones), along with Rice Bubbles, Cocoa Pops and Fruit Loops. But there were also Rice Crispies, Frosties (soooo much sugar), OKs (which got made into a savoury snack at Christmas) or Honey Smacks. Vita Brits and Weet Bix were especially good with (lots of) warm milk, and while many of my friends enjoyed a good old Weet Bix with honey after school, I always found them

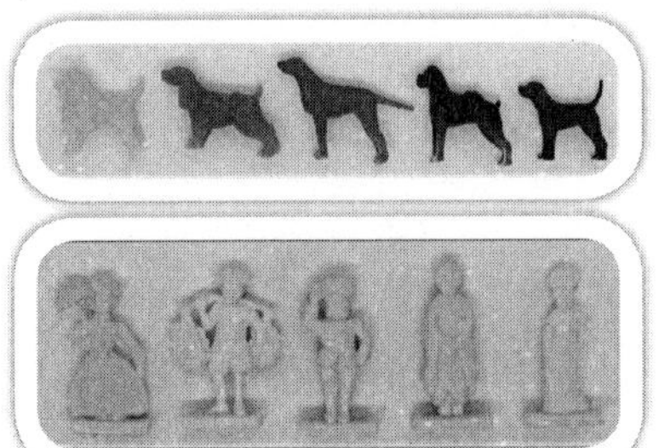

Sea Shells of the World

Where do they live?

Most shell families are widely distributed throughout the world, but each family prefers a particular environment. The nature of the shore, whether sand, pebbles, mud, rock or shingle, all count, also the roughness of the waves, the temperature and the depth of the water. Land snails and slugs live up trees or on the ground. Small winks nestle on rocks well above high tide level but where they are splashed occasionally. Limpets, chitons and ear-shells cling to rocks where waves beat and whelks hide in rock crevices and under ledges in company with octopods and squids. Many species crawl over weed beds. Some hide, others sun themselves at low tide.

Bivalves like the sandy beaches, emerging at night. Cutters near the junctions of rocks with beaches are richly populated. Sift the sand with your fingers. Some shells bore into rocks and wood while mangrove swamps well repay the searcher. Coral reefs are most exciting places. Fishermen bring up strange and beautiful shells in their nets and others are found floating on the surface of the ocean. Use your eyes well and good luck.

way too dry and hard to get through. Vita Brits had a card series to collate into a book, not unlike the Shell Petrol cards.

The waxed inner bag gave way to plastic with the catch phrase to “keep them fresh and crisp in the polythene bag”.

General dinner menus of the time were usually based around meat and three veg (usually carrots, potatoes, pumpkin, and beans if they were in season). Other veges included cabbage, peas, celery (I’d pick every single piece out), capsicum, onion and whatever Dad was growing in his vege patch at the time. We had a bean slicer, although Mum usually just topped and tailed the beans and cut them whole. Exotic things like broccoli were unheard of.

Saturday night would be roast dinner and Sunday lunch would be leftovers. Summer lunches would often be salad with ham or some other “created” meat like Devon, and I would be bribed to consume a lettuce leaf if it contained a spoonful of sugar.

Mum would vary the dinner routine with fried rice, macaroni (the ONLY pasta there was), smoked cod (that vibrantly orange stuff well drowned in white sauce), liver and bacon (stop gagging ... the way Mum made it was absolutely melt in your mouth beautiful with bacon and lots of gravy), steak and kidney pie, savoury mince on toast, pressure-cooked lamb chops, meatballs in gravy, corned beef and shepherd's pie to name a few. Chicken was a special treat usually only at Christmas or Easter, as Dad would have to kill, pluck and gut the chook first — not something he was keen to do every week.

Dessert wasn't every night, but it was delicious when it came. Apple crumble and custard, rice pudding, junket or honey milk velvet, jelly and ice cream, bottled peaches or pears, bread and butter pudding (although I wouldn't eat the soggy bread — my brother got that), or steamed puddings in winter with loads of golden syrup.

The clink of the bottles on the front porch just outside my bedroom window signalled the exchange of empty milk bottles for full ones into the wire milk bottle crate. Money that we had left out would be pocketed and the milko would be on his way back to the truck to refill for the next house.

Brisbane's one pint glass milk bottles were squarish and topped with red foil. My brother and I would compete to be the first to get the foil off so we could have the cream that had settled at the top. When homogenisation came in with its blue foil top, we felt really ripped off. Dad had a couple of rolls of the foil that had holes in where the lids had been punched out. We think he may have rescued it from the Paul's Milk factory where he worked once while he was studying. It looked great on our Christmas tree. There were plastic caps with a pouring spout that you could snap on the top of the bottles so the milk didn't get a "fridgy" taste.

To help boost up the goodness of milk (and to make it taste even better), various powders could be added. Milo, Quik, Ovaltine and Akta-Vite were favourites. Akta-Vite, developed in 1943 at Chadstone, was so good for you you could only buy it at the chemist. Captain Akta-Vite in his lycra spacesuit was part of the fixation with the space race that commercially pervaded so much of our lives. Thomas Mayne, a chemical engineer working for Nestle, developed Milo in 1934, launching it at the Sydney Royal Easter Show. He named it after Milo of Croton, an ancient Greek athlete known for his legendary strength.

With the advent of supermarkets and self-service shopping, sliced bread that came wrapped in waxed paper to help keep it fresh (and also to emblazon with branding) became the thing. With the longer "freshness" possible, it also meant that additives were included to prolong shelf life.

By 1958, Tip Top Bread offered sliced and packaged bread and became Australia's leading brand. White bread was the variety on offer. If you wanted anything else more exotic (like wholemeal) you had to make it yourself. Tip Top Bakeries was formed in 1949 by George Weston Pty Ltd when two Australian bakeries were acquired. The company went on to add more bakeries in various states.

We also had an egg man who delivered to our house. Our dog Bobby was a collie kelpie who liked to look after the fence line and round up stray visitors. Unfortunately, the egg man lost part of the back of his pants one day when he was delivering to our house ... we had to buy our eggs from the shop after that.

Other friends still had groceries delivered well into the 1960s, but I think, as we lived so close to the shops, Mum was happy to go herself to the Brisbane Cash and Carry (BCC — which was later taken over by Woolworths) and the butchers, and bring home her groceries in brown paper bags. The butchers still had the sign on the wall about "No Hawking or Expectorating", and an enormous timber block for chopping behind the counter.

Whenever "Greensleeves" plays, jingly or not, it reminds me of the bright pink Mr Whippy van slowly making its way around the street hoping for customers. The ice cream, made with skim milk and cream, had a taste all its own, and a single shilling cone was an exciting, rare treat. In 1958, Dominic Facchino from the UK had seen for himself in the US the Mr Softee ice cream trucks and brought the idea back home. 1962 saw the first Australian franchise launch in Sydney, with 200 UK-built Commer Karrier vans to follow soon after. Supposedly, Dominic had a fascination for Henry VIII, who was purported to have written "Greensleeves", hence the use of the tune and the nod to Henry's velvet cap with Mr Whippy's cap. Mr Whippy actually owns the rights to the jingly version, but no longer roams the streets, confined to markets and fairs.

With the popularity of household refrigerators and

the ability to keep things frozen, ice cream was sold in blocks or bricks wrapped up in a waxy paper or cardboard. Later it was sold in half-gallon tins. Pauls, Streets, Dairy King, Peters and Devondale were holiday treats, rationed out carefully to make the contents last. I especially liked the butterscotch brickle and would save all the little pieces of butterscotch, sucked clean of ice cream, in a ring around my bowl and eat them last. The round tins were often decorated with current themes such as Dairy King's space tin and, of course, were useful storage containers for biscuits, cakes, dead insects and rocks once emptied.

In the 1950s and 1960s, Peters Ice Cream was still "the health food of a nation", a claim that was later forced to change with new health regulations to "keeps the good things coming". Started in 1907 by American expat Fred Peters using his Mum's recipe, Peters Ice Cream began sales in Queensland in 1929 after the building of a factory at West End called Peters Arctic Delicacy. The factory was unique in that it was built without refrigeration, but used saltwater to lower the water temperature that would then freeze the ice cream.

Drum Sticks were invented in 1963 in the West End factory using cones that were made across the laneway. Problems with leaking cones led to the bright idea of bunging the end up with some chocolate. Brilliant! A Drum Stick is eaten every 1½ seconds, with over 50 million sold each year.

Pauls, originally a competitor for Peters, began in 1933 as Pauls Polar Perfections. In 1960, they joined forces to become Queensland United Foods, but still sold products under the respective brands.

Choc Wedges began in 1949, Hava Hearts in 1955, and we also had Two in Ones and Jelly Tips.

Streets, another popular ice cream brand, began in 1920 when Ted Street and his wife Daisy, in the back shed of his home at Corrimal in NSW, began making and selling ice creams and other tasty treats to his neighbours using a cart and then a one-horsepower motorbike.

Apparently, his nephew Ron, an engineer, came up with the great idea of the chocolate Paddle Pop. Ted let him run with it calling it a "nine-day wonder". This prepackaged ice cream was a brilliant alternative to the cone and scoop and could be kept in the freezer at home. Further flavours followed and the Paddle Pop Lion, who was "the lion that liked Paddle Pops", had trouble deciding which flavour to try. Introduced in 1953, this humble nine-day wonder sold over 90 million pieces by the 2000s and is the world's top selling ice cream per capita.

Streets brought us the Gaytime in 1959 — "It's hard to have a Gaytime on your own" — which was originally a strawberry ice-cream inside vanilla ice-cream and coated in a layer of chocolate and short-cake crumbs. The Golden Gaytime, toffee version, didn't appear until the 1970s.

Splice, originally Lime Splice, appeared in 1962, followed by Raspberry Splice in 1963, and in 1968, they launched Blue Ribbon Ice Cream, still a mainstay in the freezer at home.

Redskin Splits bring back memories of holidays at Coolum when there was Somer's Store on the corner and not much else. Tragedy struck if some of the red sweet outer layer fell off onto the sand. By-Jingo ice blocks were another favourite on hot summer days.

Sunny-boys, in their unique pyramid Tetrapak, were a big part of school tuckshop life. It was a real struggle to get it finished

before the end of lunchtime unless you were lucky and they weren't frozen rock solid to start with. The orange syrup always seemed to settle to one side of the block. Berri Limited brought out the super sweet orange flavoured ice treat in 1964.

If you ask for a lolly in Britain, you will be handed an icy pole. In Australia, you will be presented with a plethora of sweet treats from Smarties to Wild Raspberries, chocolates being a completely different animal. As kids, the local lolly shop, conveniently located outside the back gate of our school, was heaven, with rows of open boxes filled with gloriously unwrapped treats positioned at eye height underneath glass topped and fronted counters. The ubiquitous white bag would be filled with "one of those" and "three of these". God bless the shopkeepers who, using their fingers, picked out the requested lollies, counting up the pennies or cents as they went. We didn't even notice the dead blowies, lying legs up between the box and the glass.

Fags (now politically correct Fads without the red glowing end), love hearts with special messages that made up for the lack of flavour, cobbers (the unwrapped version of Fantales), milk bottles, false teeth, bananas, clinkers, snifters, fizzers, black cats, chicos, freckles, musk sticks, bullets, spearmint leaves, and lolly necklaces that draped around your neck and acquired a tangy salty flavor by the end of the day while the colours lost a bit of their purity.

The wrapped, and a little more expensive ones included Milkos, Red Skins, Pascall Fruit Bon Bons, Sherbet Cones (with a licorice straw), White Knights, Steamrollers, Choo Choo Bars, Lemon Sherbets, Lifesavers and Fruit Tingles.

Bubble gum was a chapter in itself with Black Cat (licorice flavour), Big Tooth bubble gum that came in a giant plastic tooth, Scanlan's Metro, Bazooka, Big Charlie and Bellboy. You could get chewing gum in little packs of three or four — Wrigley's Juicy Fruit, PK or Spearmint. Apparently, PK was named for Phillip Knight Wrigley, or P K as he was known. Full size Wrigley's also included Spearmint, Arrowmint and

Double Mint. I couldn't handle the spearmint flavours after a long session with Bis Pectin when I contracted gastro at the tender age of five.

Kid-oriented chocolates were Milky Bar, Yogi Bear ("Start at the knees please"), Bertie Beetles that used up the leftover bits from the Violet Crumbles, and Freddos (originally, they were going to be mice).

Adults had their share with MacRobertson's Snack chocolate block or tins of mixed chocolates, Red Tulip After Dinner Mints (launched in 1965 and THE thing to have with dinner guests), Polly Waffle, Picnic Bar (1958), Black Cat Chocolate box, Cherry Ripes (1924), Crunchies, Violet Crumble and Old Gold.

Mastercraft chocolates offered Golden Rough and Milky Way, as well as their Scorched Peanut Bar.

MacRobertson's was founded by Sir Macpherson Robertson in 1880, originally making boiled lollies. By 1940, MacRobertson's was Australia's biggest chocolate manufacturer and was eventually sold to Cadbury in 1967.

Red Tulip chocolates were started in 1939 by the Nassau family, Jewish immigrants who made the chocolates in their home in Caulfield. They too were bought out by Cadbury in 1980.

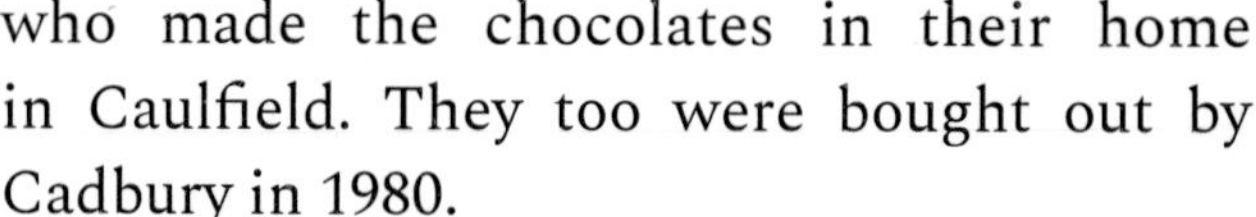

Allen's Sweets owner, Alfred Allen, originally worked for Macpherson Robertson until branching out on his own in 1891. By 1903, his company was the third largest confectionery company in Melbourne and today, now owned by Nestle, is the top sugar confectionery brand in Australia.

Starting business as the Rising Sun Preserving Works and producing jams, preserves and confectionery, Hoadley's Chocolates was formed in 1913 when Henry

Jones Co-operative Ltd acquired the jam business. Violet Crumble bars, created in 1913, were named in honour of Mrs Hoadley's favourite flower. Hoadley's merged with Rowntree in 1970 and is now owned by Nestle.

Sweetacres was the name given to the new factory where James Stedman-Henderson moved the manufacture of his Lion Brand Confectionery, changing the name to Sweetacres. Minties (1922), Jaffas (1931) and Fantales (1939) were made here. Life-savers, an American lolly, were introduced to Australia by Sweetacres. The company was taken over by Hoadley's, and is now owned by Allen's.

Plaistowe was started in Perth in 1915 creating the famous Choo Choo Bar that stained tongues and teeth for generations. Plaistowe is now owned by Nestle, but you will still see the brand name on cocoa and cooking chocolate. The Choo Choo Bar is now made by Lagoon Confectioners.

There was, of course, the homemade yummies that were sold at school fetes and church fairs. Vibrant coconut ice, chocolate fudge (Mum's was THE best), marshmallow, honeycomb, peanut brittle, toffees in the paper patty cake holders with sprinkles on the top, and the toffee apple on a stick that became a dangerous weapon after it was all eaten clean. Russian toffee was delicious, and Dad had a recipe that was in the form of a poem. All the recipes kept CSR smiling and rubbing their hands, while the dental fraternity watched and polished their little surgical mirrors.

Here we must make mention of Easter eggs which we ONLY got to consume on Easter Sunday AFTER we'd been to church. My husband remembers scoffing all of his in a very short space of time while his sister savoured hers and kept them almost until they turned white ... or he found them.

Red Tulip (owned by Cadbury since 1980) chocolate eggs had a glorious special taste that just seems to have disappeared. It used to be a not-too-sweet not-too-bitter smooth chocolate, but now they seem to taste like any other Cadbury chocolate bar. Such a shame! And if anyone tried to pass one of those shameful excuses for an Easter egg — the sugar egg — onto me, I was totally devastated. They had the taste and consistency of plaster of Paris ... most disappointing.

Maggi and Continental dried soups hit the shelves in the early part of the 1950s and everyone learned how to make French onion soup dip for their soirees, placed decorously alongside the devils on horseback (prunes wrapped in bacon) and the incredible selection of wobbly things encased in gelatin. Chicken noodle packet soup was included in Chinese-oriented recipes.

In 1897, the general manager of the United States company Campbell's did the right thing and hired his nephew, a chemist who was really keen to join Campbell's. He ended up revolutionising soup by developing condensed soup and throwing it into a can. Campbell's entered the Australian market in 1964, opening a manufacturing facility at Shepparton Victoria. Andy Warhol painted his first can of Campbell's soup in 1962, apparently because he liked soup. I am sure Campbell's liked Andy Warhol too!

Birds Eye released fish fingers in 1956, supposedly to tempt children to eat more fish. And while Vegemite had been around for yonks, we became Happy Little Vegemites with the song penned by Alan Weekes in 1954.

We were fortunate that the fast food epidemic (read KFC and Maccas) didn't really cross the border until the very late 1960s, early 1970s.

In 1951, Frank McEnroe, a boilermaker from Bendigo, was doing his thing selling food at the local footy matches and developed a deep-fried treat based on a Chinese chop suey roll. This was to become the iconic Chiko Roll. It got such a following that he ventured out and tested the market at the Wagga Agricultural Show in 1951. The rest is history! What is a Chiko Roll made of? Cabbage, lots of cabbage, barley, carrot, green beans, beef, celery and onion, all wrapped up in a thick egg and flour casing and deep fried. Oh, and did I mention it has cabbage in it?

Commercially made savoury snack foods would appear at parties or Christmas, and weren't the small, dubiously named "single serve" packs that proliferate in children's lunch boxes today. In 1950, cheese Twisties were developed by Isador Magid, who imported a rotary head extruder from the USA. He sold the name and machine to Monty Lea of Darrell Lea fame, who had better success turning Twisties into an iconic Australian snack. It then went to Smith's Snackfoods.

Red Seal Chips, that were "good'n'crisp", were manufactured by Freer's Superfoods, a company started by Gerard Freer in 1960 manufacturing chips and other food lines in Herston, Brisbane. The damaged chips from the production line were fed to the cows in the neighbouring paddock. Panda Potato Crisps were "as good for you as home cooked potatoes and starch reduced" and were also made at Herston.

Smith's was founded in the UK by Frank Smith and Jim Viney in 1920, setting up in Australia in 1931. After a financially tumultuous time with the Depression, post war saw rapid growth. In 1960, they were producing a one shilling pack for the movie theatre or a boxed pack for four shillings. 1961 saw the introduction of chips with chicken flavouring. It was so popular that other companies felt the need to imitate it. Although Australians know them as chips, Smith's were still using the UK name of crisps until the early 2000s. I find chip packets just don't burst as well as they used to.

Wartime rationing was only just coming to a close in 1950, with butter and tea being the final ones to finish in June and July (respectively) of that year. Dripping had been the staple instead of butter, so it was a relief for many to be able to ply their toast with butter again. With only clothing, tea, sugar, butter, meat and occasionally eggs and milk rationed, Australia had not had to bear the brunt of such intense rationing as Britain.

Margarine and butter had been fighting a battle for years, with the dairy farm lobby voicing concerns over the potential of margarine to take over butter sales. Government margarine production quotas per company were enforced, along with various legislation in different states regarding the prevention of yellow colouring being added to the white product to ensure it didn't look like butter. Fortunately, it didn't go so far as one state in America, which enforced a pink colouring for margarine.

Meadow Lea, begun by Oliver Triggs in 1932, was the first margarine to be sold in Australia as a table product. As the quota wars heated up, in 1961, Marrickville (started in 1908 by Charles Abel using peanut oil) launched Miracle, a polyunsaturated table margarine based on safflower oil as a serious competitor. Cholesterol and polyunsaturated fats were getting consumer attention at the time, and Miracle led the market for a while. In our fridge, we had DixieBell margarine in its square, heavy plastic container. The containers were in a range of colours and served long duty sitting uniformly in Mum's sewing cabinet holding buttons, pins and other bits and bobs.

Brisbane had its own soft drink brands like Wimmer's, Tristram's, Horitz, Crystal and Osborne that were delivered to your house (not ours!) in wooden crates. The Tristram's truck would drive straight past our house, much to our disgust, especially if they stopped outside a neighbour's place. Bottles would be returned much like milk bottles and re-used more than 25 times. Soft drinks at our place were relegated to Christmas time or very special occasions, for which, in truth, I am rather glad. Other soft drink names of the time were Tresca, Tarax, Leed, Kirks and 7up. Of course, Coke and Pepsi were there too, with Coca Cola beginning production here in 1937 (although bottles had been arriving by ship since the early 1900s). Pepsi didn't turn up until 1951. Interestingly, Coca Cola had the opportunity three times to buy out Pepsi in the 1920s and 1930s and declined.

In the 1950s, Australia had around 600 soft drink makers, many of them small family-owned bottling companies that were sucked up into larger corporations or simply disappeared, unable to compete with infrastructure, finance and marketing knowhow. Vending machines started popping up in the early 1950s, with bottles standing in iced water rather than the upright versions we now have.

With the advent of weight loss hysteria, Royal Crown Cola in the States developed the first sugar-free cola and sales took off. Not to be out done, in 1963, Coca Cola launched Tab soda (sweetened initially with cyclamate and saccharin) for those who wanted to keep a "tab" on their weight. The original logo had a swirly a in the TaB, giving

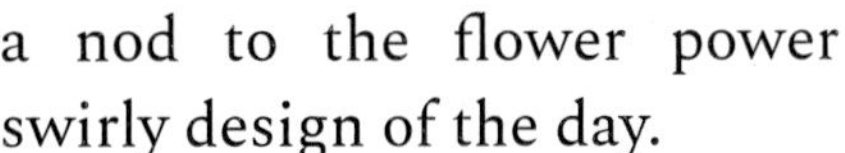

a nod to the flower power swirly design of the day.

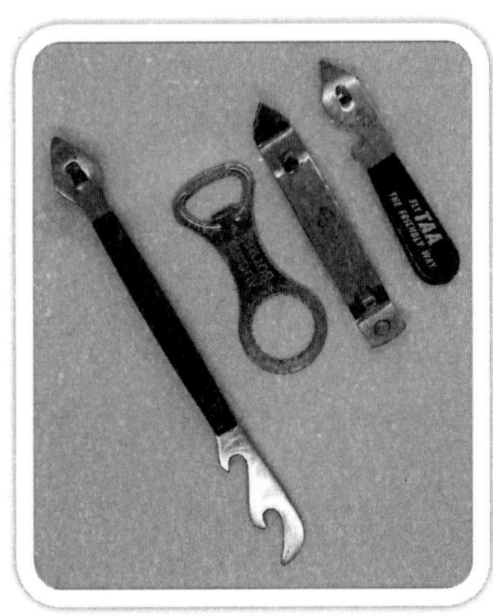

Canning of soft drinks started in Australia in 1961 using a "church-key" to open them, making two triangular holes in the top. The ring pull didn't come to our shores until Swan Brewery in Perth began to use them in 1969. Anyone growing up in the

1970s will remember the litter of ring tops that lay everywhere. Of course, the more creative in the community developed artistic uses for them like the classic ring pull necklace — never really took off!!

Tang orange-flavoured drink, which you made up from a powder, became popular. I am sure it was 99 per cent sugar, but NASA had used it on their 1962 and Gemini flights so it must have been good for you. Whenever you later asked for an orange juice at the pub, it tasted suspiciously of Tang.

Not that I knew anything about it ('til much later), but in 1965, Tom Angove of Angove Wines in Renmark, South Australia, invented the wine cask (another amazing Australian invention). Originally it was just a gallon bag where you cut the corner off and used a peg to reseal it. It wasn't until 1967, when it was developed further by Penfolds and Charles Malpas, that a plastic airtight tap was welded to a bladder. Legendary!!!

Screw-top soft drink bottles hadn't appeared yet, and the tops of the bottles had to be popped off with a bottle opener. They were lined with cork to help with the seal. When larger, family-sized bottles arrived on the scene, a screw-top lid became essential to keep the contents from going flat. Nowadays, our screw-top lids split when you open them, so you know the drink hasn't been tampered with — something we never really considered back then.

Mum used to always have a good supply of homemade biscuits. In fact, one of my friends, years later, said she loved coming to my place because there were always nice homemade biscuits to eat — found out her priorities, didn't I? Of course, we would usually have some commercial biscuits lurking in case visitors came and the kids had cleaned the biscuit container out.

I loved it when there were Arnott's Assorted Cream biscuits, and would sneak one of each kind into a bag before I headed out on my scooter. Arnott's, and its feathered parrot, has captured the Australian biscuit market since 1888 with household names such as Jatz, Ginger Nuts, SAOs, Milk Arrowroots, Lemon Lattice, Spicy Fruit Roll (or pillow biscuits — never my favourite), Nice, Scotch Fingers, Iced Vovos and Monte Carlos. Of course, there were the scandalous Golliwog biscuits, which were later named Scalliwags, and then disappeared off the shelves.

Tim Tams, arguably Arnott's most popular biscuit, started out in 1963 and were named in honour of a horse that ran in the Kentucky Derby in 1958. Ross Arnott had been at the race and took a liking to the name.

Many smaller biscuit manufacturers in Australia were consumed by either Arnott's or other international conglomerates, or Arnott's took over some of the international biscuit varieties.

Weston's, a British biscuit firm, is best known for its Wagon Wheels. This iconic biscuit was thought up in 1948 and began selling here in 1952 (in open bags) when Garry Weston moved over here and set up the Australian branch of the Weston Biscuit Company. His father George, biscuit baron, had the motto, "People will eat horse*&% if it has enough icing on it". A true entrepreneur.

Peek Frean, a UK company, established itself in Australia in 1934, producing well-known favourites such as Vita Wheat (the ones you could squeeze together and make butter and vegemite worms), Marie, Cream Wafers and Custard Creams. This was the company that pioneered chocolate-coated biscuits, and for that we should all be eternally grateful. They too were swallowed up by Arnott's in 1975.

I have to make mention of the Girl Guide biscuits that we looked forward to each year when they were sold door-to-door by Guides and Brownies (including me). They were so delicious and, while they are still available, they just aren't quite the same — or maybe my tastebuds have "matured". Still love them though!

To accompany your biscuit (certainly NOT called a cookie) was the good old cuppa tea (certainly NOT the teabag type). Tea leaves

(certainly NOT anything but black tea) would be measured into the pot ("One for each person and one for the pot", which as my father pointed out was pretty dumb, as teapots all hold different amounts of water), boiling water from the buttery yellow Hotpoint ceramic electric jug (the kind with the element that you could replace) would be poured in, and then a tea cosy plopped over the pot to keep it warm. Tea cosies were many and varied and often of the knitted kind, although there were quilted ones, embroidered ones and even lacy ones if you were really fancy shmancy. Some had doll heads with or without torsos and were downright creepy.

Lan Choo ("The favourite tea with most housewives"), Billy Tea, Tetley (arriving on our shores in 1963) and Bushells (which dominated the market) were household names. Australians were still recovering from the tea rationing of World War II as the supplies from the Dutch East Indies had been seriously interrupted. It wasn't until July 1950 that it was lifted, and Australians could celebrate with more than their daily wartime ration of around three weak cups a day.

My step-gran, being a prim tea drinker, would only keep Bushells Coffee and Chicory Essence in her cupboard for those people (like me) who wanted something different. During the 1930s, chicory was used as a coffee substitute during the Depression years and Bushells added this to their range.

Although coffee was a good alternative to the heavily rationed tea during World War II, it wasn't really until the 1950s, with the influx of European immigrants and their espresso abilities, that coffee started to become the popular drink it is today. Instant coffee like Pablo, International Roast, Bushells and Maxwell House were on the market, with Nestle manufacturing its famous Nescafe in Dennington Victoria from 1947. Instant coffee was marketed on the grounds of economy and ease, even easier than the good old-fashioned, conservative tea.

Nigger Boy Licorice was made in Caulfield, Victoria by National Licorice Pty

Ltd which was an American company. It was a big feature of the show bags at the Royal Show and contained an assortment of different types of licorice, including licorice rope and King Size Cigarettes ("The safe smoke for junior"). The name was changed in the early 1960s to Lucky Boy licorice. "Nigger boy gives endless joy!" Obviously entirely inappropriate and offensive now and also then.

WELCOME...

to the ROYAL SHOW

NIGGER BOY . . . hopes you have a **HAPPY TIME!**

One of the most popular attractions is . . .

NIGGER BOY'S SAMPLE BAG

. . . because it gives you the most **VALUE**

NIGGER BOY LICORICE is good for your health

You will enjoy its wholesome, nourishing goodness at all times.

YOU TOO WILL SAY . . .

"I Love Nigger Boy"

You will always know **NIGGER BOY** products by the famous **NIGGER BOY** picture on every pack sold through the year everywhere

- **3/- T.V. Pack**—"Chew while you View".
- **2/6 Family Pack**—The original and ever popular family carton.
- **1/6 Slimming Licorice**—For Mum and Sis too. A doctor has advised that Licorice is a slimming aid.
- **9d. and 1/- Soft Eating Licorice**—Contains a colourful card.
- **6d. King Size Cigarettes**—The safe smoke for junior.
- **6d. Licorice Rope**—A yard of super soft, most popular Licorice Rope.
- **3d. Monsters**—15 ins. of thick chewy twist.
- **1d. Licorice Novelties**—Big variety of favourites adored by children.
- **4 @ 1d. Licorice and Aniseed Blox**—The ever popular chew sweet.
- **1/- Pack Licorice Allsorts.** (The Edinburgh Brand). Also sold at 5 ozs. for 1/-.

INSIST ON THE BRAND — ASK FOR THEM BY NAME AND LEARN THAT . . .

"NIGGER BOY GIVES ENDLESS JOY"

Manufactured by **NATIONAL LICORICE PTY. LTD.,**
42-58 Hawthorn Road, Caulfield, Vic. Phone: 50-8439.

If your shop nearby does not stock Nigger Boy Products tell us the Shop's name.
If you are the first we will send you a free packet of licorice.

I LOVE NIGGER BOY

Stuff we had in the laundry

Concrete double laundry tubs were the norm and were such a far cry from the clean, shiny, smooth stainless steel tubs that now grace our laundries. They were rough, cold and unforgiving, but did the job. Our house had an electric copper that was wired into the electrical circuit. Each week, Mum would wash all the sheets and towels in there, heating up the water and shaving sunlight soap into it. She would wait until it cooled and then, using her long wooden "copper stick", heave the wet material into the sink filled with clean water where she would rinse. The stick was replaced a few years later with spring loaded pine tongs.

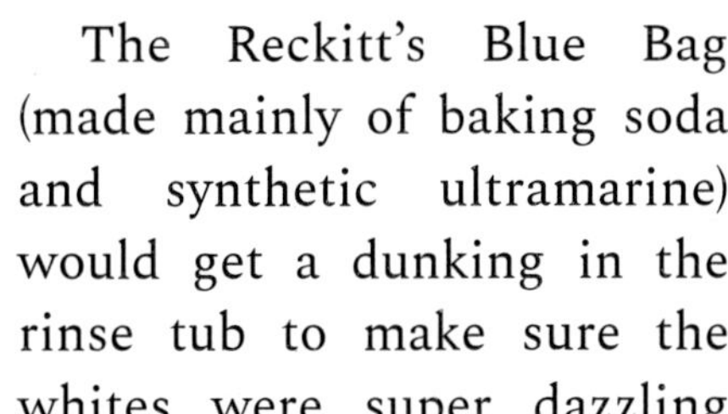

The Reckitt's Blue Bag (made mainly of baking soda and synthetic ultramarine) would get a dunking in the rinse tub to make sure the whites were super dazzling white. Then it was into the wringer (or later, the spinner) before emptying the copper of water, which I always thought looked pretty goopy and a bit mucilaginous. But our sheets and towels were always super clean.

Our original washing machine was a Pope wringer that Mum had been given by a friend who won it in a competition but didn't want it — big win for Mum and Dad! When it finally died, Dad removed the engine for other greater purposes and used the tub to make a fish tank in our bush house. We stocked it with guppies that we happily fed with mosquito larvae retrieved from our mossy forest birdbath using Mum's tea strainer. It was also here that the concrete tubs found their final resting place, filled with potting mix and baby ferns that sprouted in the damp. Pope Products, founded in South Australia in 1935, initially manufactured irrigation products, but today are best remembered for their wringer washing machine.

Ours had the electric wringer, but earlier models were the hand-operated mangle. There are, of course, innumerable gory tales of hands, arms and hair getting caught and going through the wringer. I even read of a case where a woman got her left boob caught in one — perhaps she had burnt her bra a bit early! Improvements were made and there was a safety mechanism that would pop the rollers apart if something got caught.

Twin tubs started taking over from the wringers in the 1960s, and although they were still time-consuming, they were a lot more efficient than the wringer. As they were not plumbed in, they had to be filled manually. Often the laundry tap was a bi-fold one that could cover a fair distance. One tub was for washing and the other for spinning. Water from the wash or rinse load could be pumped, using an attached hose, into the laundry tub to be repumped back into the machine to use for the next load. Invariably, if you weren't watching, the hose would flick out of the sink and pump water all over the floor.

You can still buy twin tubs, but I am happy to stick with my automatic number. I have a picture above my washing machine of my grandmother in 1915, slaving away over the copper outside on a fire. I don't complain (too much) about having to do the laundry.

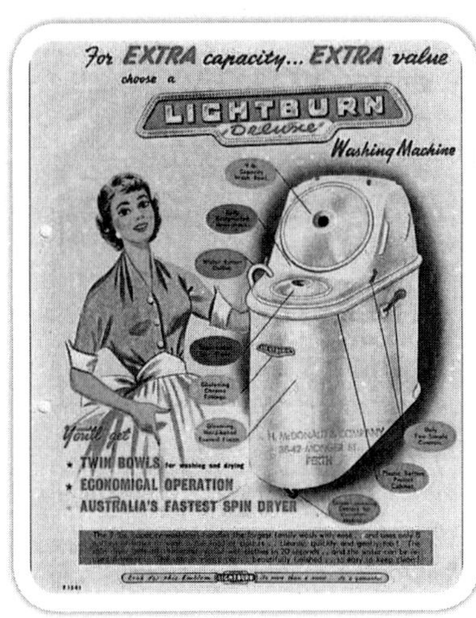

The Lightburn washing machine was another electric twin tub machine that was popular in areas with less water supply or in multi-use places like caravan parks or the Australian Army. The body and the washing bowl were fibreglass while the spin bowl was steel. Lightburn, a South Australian company, began selling their washing machine in 1949. They were also well known for Lightning brand cement mixers, and perhaps less well known for their ill-fated venture into making the fibreglass Zeta car in 1963. With a two-stroke engine, Perspex windows and steel doors, it only sold around 400 by the time it finished up in 1966.

Everyone wanted whiter than white whites, especially now that it was easier with the electric washers doing the work. White King began its career in Australia in the 1950s as a liquid bleach, expanding into providing cleaners for every room.

Surf washing powder offered us the "World's Cleanest Wash" with the "same wonderful results even in hard water".

Omo, first registered in the UK around 1908, was launched onto the Australian market by Unilever in 1954 aiming at both the "boiling market" and the "washing machine market". Blue Omo came not long after, adding even more whiteness to whites and brightness to colours — "the brightness women want". Legend has it that Omo stands for "Old Mother Owl", suggesting you were making a wise choice when you purchased it.

Rinso was one of the first mass-marketed soap powders and had already been around for quite a while. The big catchcry for Rinso was the ability to soak the clothes in it before washing, making no need for rubbing or scrubbing, "and no backache". It was meant to "make colours brighter and wash

clothes whiter than new" (sound familiar?). During the late 1950s, "the Rinso kids", a family of 10, were used in advertising as the healthiest, happiest and cleanest in Australia. Things weren't as "perfect" in reality, and within a year of the advertisement, Mum, with Dad in prison, couldn't keep up with the rent and her children were removed by welfare officers.

Persil was another longstanding laundry detergent developed in 1907. The name is made up of two of its magic ingredients — sodium perborate (bleach) and silicate (base washing agent). This created what they called a "self-activating powder detergent" and the "amazing oxygen washer" due to the action of the sodium perborate creating little bubbles. "Your first time means a Persil dazzle thrill." Woohoo. Glad we are talking about washing powder here.

Hospital woollen blankets came under fire in the 1960s, suspected of harbouring nasty germs as they couldn't be laundered in hot water. CSIRO's Tom Pressley formulated a method using a shrink-proofing process that allowed washing at 80 °C, but the blankets became rough after lots of washes. He then set about developing a special detergent to use with woollen fabrics and Softly was born, and the Australian wool industry sighed a collective sigh.

Lux Flakes, another laundry detergent for woollens, was really just flakes of Sunlight soap.

Many houses of the time had polished timber floors with, perhaps, the kitchen and laundry floors covered with lino. Wall-to-wall carpeting was only for the very wealthy, and at that stage was usually strips of carpet laid side by side rather than broadloom. There were loose carpets and rugs instead. Mum would polish the timber floor with O'Cedar oil and a big heavy floor polisher, and, in between, wipe it over with a big soft cotton mop.

The 1960s saw a love of shag carpet infiltrate, and for a while, it was the epitome of a modern home being the complete antithesis to the sensible low pile carpeting of the past. The shag style stretched across into the fake fur that was plastered on everything from cushions to toilet lids. It began to fall out of favour again when people realised how difficult it was to maintain and keep clean, although it didn't stop Jayne Mansfield lining her whole bathroom in pink shag.

When Mum and Dad married, one thing she asked for was an electric vacuum cleaner. She got it! An Electrolux square barrelled monster that lasted many years. Vacuum cleaner salesmen still came door to door in those days, but weren't able to convince Mum to relinquish hers.

The world's first clean-air upright vacuum cleaner, the Hoover Dynamatic, was released in 1963. With this development, adopted by many other manufacturers and still being used, dirt would no longer pass through the suction fan first, but would pass through the bag leaving clean air to pass through the fan.

With the space race well and truly taking hold of imaginations, Hoover launched its Constellation in 1952 — "the cleaner that walks on air" floating on its exhaust like a hovercraft.

Samuel Taylor Pty Ltd launched Australia's aerosol industry in 1953 with the Pressure Pak, and offered the first aerosol-based cleaning product in Australia in the late 1950s. I think everyone remembers the cute little Mr Sheen with his big glasses and rosy cheeks as he slid his bottom across tabletops and down banister rails ("Clean, wax and polish as you dust with Mr Sheen"). Mr Sheen was reputed to have been "modelled" on one of the employees (I wonder if he ever found out). Incidentally,

Samuel Taylor Pty Ltd was also responsible for the Mortein Pressure Pak.

Brisbane's tap water was notoriously hard, making a good lather up not an easy thing. Our house had a water softener installed. Softeners worked on an ion exchange where, as the water passed through, tiny resin beads would remove the calcium and magnesium. Part of Dad's job was to flush it through every few weeks with brine to regenerate the beads. The added benefit of a softener was that it helped to reduce the buildup of lime scale in the plumbing. I recall when it had to be replaced, Dad opened up the old softener and we marvelled at the little golden beads inside. I think they were whisked away before we could do anything too exciting with them.

In 1945, Lance Hill of Adelaide made a new washing line for his wife, with extra line space and more stability than her current prop washing line. His neighbours loved it so he built some for them too. He purchased salvaged tubing that had been hung under the Sydney Harbour Bridge during WWII to catch enemy subs to make his first orders. In 1947, making use of an expired 1925 patent (Gilbert Toyne of Geelong) for a crown wheel-and-pinion winding mechanism, he started to manufacture the wind-up rotary clothes hoist. It has become a recognised Australian cultural icon and is listed as a National Treasure by the National Library of Australia. More than five million Hills Hoists are sold each year around the world.

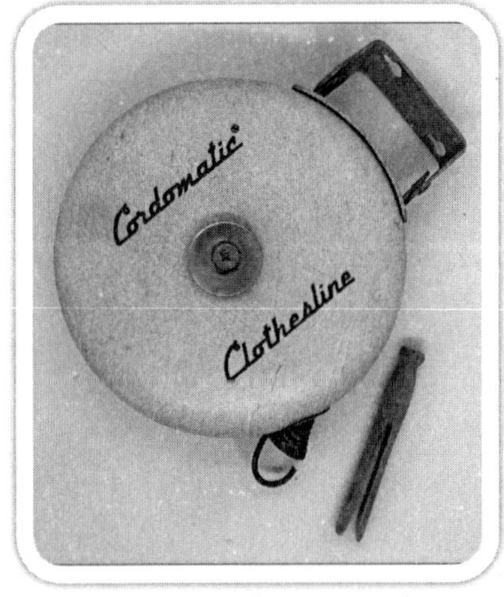

Of course, where space was limited, a Hills Hoist just wouldn't work, so clever Hills put out the retractable Cordomatic clothesline, ensuring that they had complete market coverage.

Clothing was pegged out to dry with wooden dolly pegs. Dolly pegs were often used by children to make dollies to play with, dressing them up and drawing faces on the "heads". Australia's main dolly peg supply came from a factory built by Pioneer Woodware Company in New Norfolk, Tasmania in 1926, which made around 1.4 million sassafras wooden pegs a week.

Disaster struck in 1948 when the factory burnt down, requiring an interim factory to be set up capable of only producing square pegs. A new factory was built in 1949, and 10 years later, the company began manufacturing wooden pegs with springs. The spring peg, although invented way back in 1853 in the US, didn't really take over our clotheslines until the 1960s. The Derwent River flooded in 1960, causing massive damage to the peg factory. Coupled with one of those government decisions to remove import duties allowing cheap foreign pegs to flood the Australian market, the factory closed its doors in 1975.

There were lots of things to iron, especially as a lot of the fabric used was cotton before polyester came on the scene — school uniforms, work shirts and trousers, dresses, pillowcases and tea towels. Thankfully, Mum never went so far as ironing the sheets or undies (which meant I never had to either!).

Before the steam iron hit the market, things had to be damped down, rolled up and left to sit for a while. Water was sprinkled from soft drink bottles with holes drilled in corks or flicked over by hand. That is, until Tupperware came up with the perforated lid for their tall cups, which did the same job but were so much more modern and decorous.

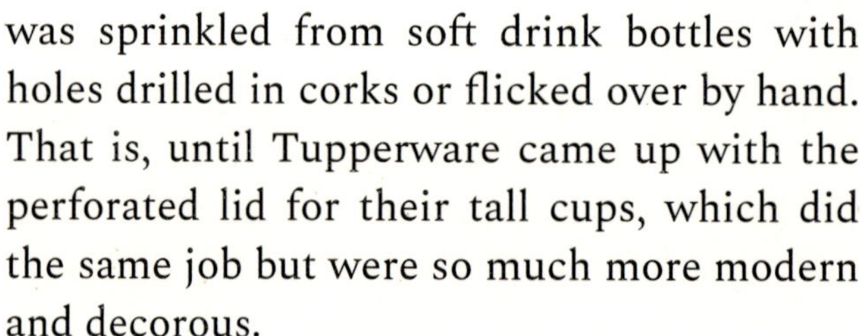

Many irons still didn't have a thermostat so it was a matter of turning it on and off at the wall when it got too hot. My introduction to ironing was doing the hankies — there were always quite a few (we didn't go in for tissues at that stage). Dad's and my brother's were folded into a square, Mum's into a rectangle and mine ended up as a triangle. Not sure if there was any mystical deep reasoning for this. We didn't have much that needed starching, preferring seersucker tablecloths to the fussy linen ones, although Fabulon spray starch found its way into the ironing basket for Dad's work shirts.

To start with we had a little triangular GE Hotpoint that didn't have a thermostat. From there, we moved up in the world to a thermostatically controlled Hecla, and it wasn't until much later that we purchased a Sunbeam steam iron (from RT Edwards at Greenslopes — a whole family adventure!).

The laundry cupboard always had a rag bag with clothes that were way beyond repair for use in the shed with painting or other dirty work, like polishing silver, brass or shoes. When sheets got thin in the middle, Mum would split them up the centre and sew the sides together to get a bit more mileage out of them. When they were completely knackered, she would diligently tear them into long strips, roll them up and pass them on to the Leprosy Mission.

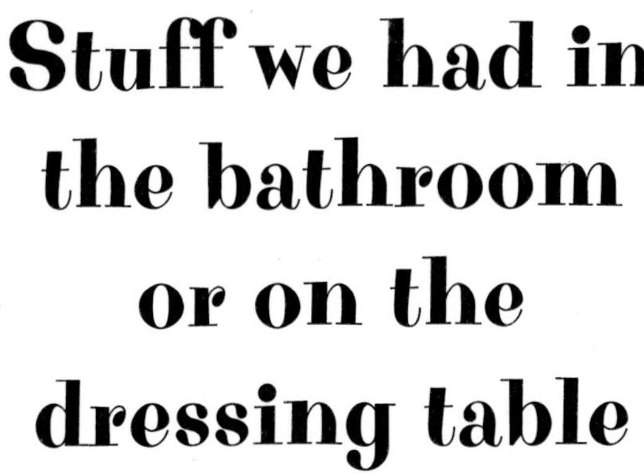

Stuff we had in the bathroom or on the dressing table

Being built in the early 1950s, our bathroom at Mt Gravatt was the classic 50s bathroom with terrazzo floor, green porcelain bath and handbasin, with a little wooden cabinet on the wall. The walls were pale pink, fake tile sheeting made from Masonite, and we had a shower rose over the bath with a curtain rail that ran around it. We didn't actually use the shower as Dad was worried that the Masonite would get wet and swell and have to be replaced. He religiously wiped along the bottom edge every night after we had had our baths to make sure no moisture got into it. It wasn't until we had renovations done to build in a flushing toilet that we also had a shower cubicle put in — we then became consistent shower users.

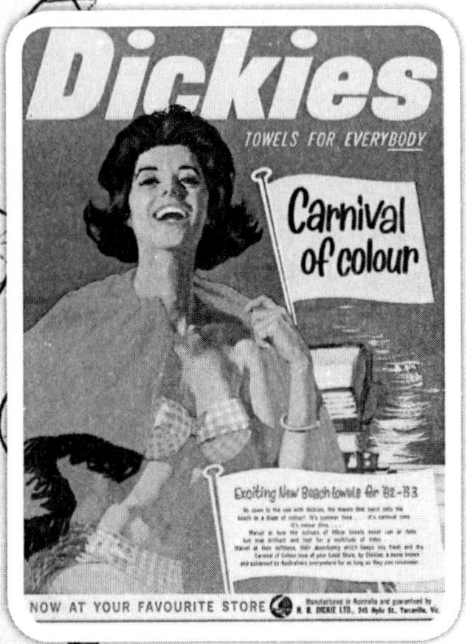

Before we started accepting a lot of cheaper imported

towels, Dri-Glo and Dickies were the mainstays in most people's bathrooms.

Made in Australia since 1927 at the weaving mill first in Yarraville and then in Wangaratta, they are the iconic Aussie brands in the bathroom.

Soaps were many and varied, from disinfecting to

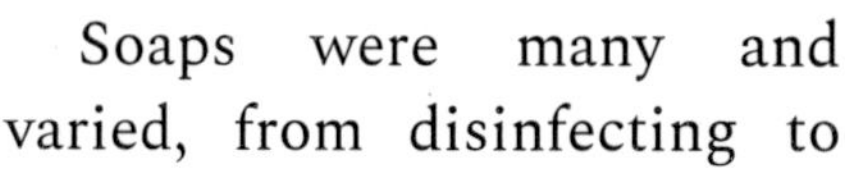

plain Jane to luxury soaps that the movie stars used. We used Gamophen, which was a germ killer but smelt quite nice. Solyptol soap was another in the germ removal brigade.

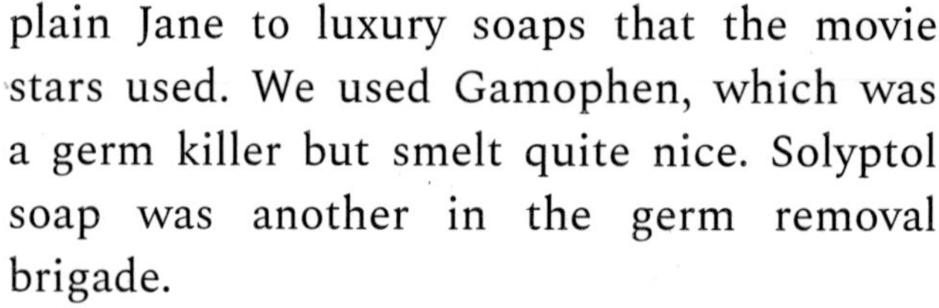

If we were given special soaps for our birthday or Christmas, they usually got shoved into our undies drawer to make them smell good, and by the end they had no smell left and had changed colour.

Sunlight soap was the go-to for everything — clothes, hair, body, hands, kitchen sink, dogs — everything. Originally made in the UK in 1884, it was the very first soap to be imprinted and packaged. In fact, it was so successful over there that the Lever Brothers made their very own village for its workers to live in called Port Sunlight. In 1895, they opened a soap factory in Balmain, New South Wales. Lux Soap, Country Life,

Camay, Yardley, Velvet, Lifebuoy, Palmolive, Cashmere Bouquet and Rexona were all well known. I'm not sure how they tasted, but my brother has a recollection of a couple from when he was in kindy to help with his choice of vocabulary.

Avon, Bronnley and Potter & Moore had a plethora of shaped soaps as both guest soaps and personal soaps. They were a popular item at Christmas time, with gift boxes for both children and adults left to proliferate in drawers as they were just too nice to use.

Soap on a rope was supposedly added to the English Leather Company's catalogue in the early 1950s, but I have heard a rumour that it was invented in prison (I'll leave that one to your imagination). At any rate, it became a popular gift for fathers during the 1960s. Avon caught on to the idea and made all sorts of shaped soap connected to a bit of rope.

We had sponges to wash ourselves with — green for the boys and pink for the girls.

Men's cologne was called the more manly term of "aftershave", but really, aside from some minimal medicinal value, it just made them smell nice. English Leather had held sway since 1949, while Old Spice had been around since 1938 in its buoy-shaped bottle. It was a mainstay in the Christmas gift department, especially as a gift for a male teacher. Tabac was available from 1959 while Faberge's Brut came out in 1964.

Fortunately, perfumes had moved on from the lavender water of old. Classics like Chanel No 5, Youth Dew and Jon Patou's Joy were advertised in magazines, but were beyond the reach of the mortal suburban mum. 4711, Avon and Yardley came to the rescue with not only more moderate pricing, but Avon had exciting bottle shapes to boot. I had a particularly beautiful Avon glass bell perfume bottle with a gold handle. The perfume went off pretty quickly, but the bottle looked gorgeous on my dressing table. Mums were asked "Are you wearing Tweed?" Escapade perfume, in 1953, could help you "express your gayest self", and Avon's Unforgettable was, well, unforgettable. Tabu was the forbidden fragrance by Dana, who also produced Ambush, "the woman's tactic", while Faberge produced Tigress, which turned you into a man hunter.

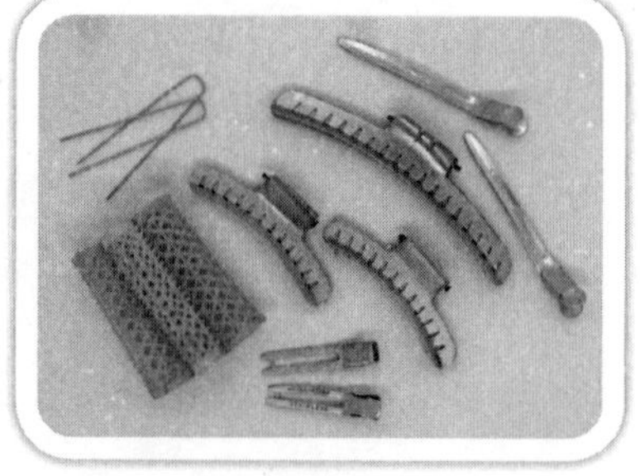

Whenever Mum washed her hair, which was already wavy, she would set it with metal wave clips. They were ferocious beasts with sharp teeth and tight springs, and hurt like blazes if you clamped them on your finger (tests of fortitude with my brother). My hair was thick and STRAIGHT, and no amount of crimping or curling would last long, try as we might. We would attempt ringlets now and then, tightly wrapping my hair in lengths of cotton sheeting. Sleeping was minimal those nights. Pink hair setting gel would come out if we were trying to secure curls but, disappointingly, they all fell out way too soon.

With the long hair came the battles after it was washed to comb it out. It was torture until Mum came across conditioner in the local hair salon. I think it was Delva, an Australian brand, and came in a plastic bottle that looked like cut glass and smelled like crushed chrysanthemums. I hated it. However, because it made the process less onerous, I put up with it.

Unless you could afford to go to the hair salon, you had to set your hair at home before bed using rollers, cover them with a hair net or scarf and then try to sleep in them. Domestic hair dryers just weren't a thing. Then a portable soft-bonnet version of the big pull-down canopies at the hair salon became available and you could dry your hair in under half an hour.

Hairstyles of big sisters or, in my case, older cousins, included the bouffant style where the hair was wound around rollers and encapsulated in one of those hooded dryers for hours. When it was finally dry, it was back-combed to give it height and then sprayed with copious amounts of hairspray. The other style was the beehive, which originated in Chicago as a variety of the bouffant. It was more of a cone shape and resembled, well, a beehive. It was also compared to the nose cone of the B52 airplane. The teacher next to our class in Grade One, Miss Andrews, would sport one or the other of these at school.

Of course, as a helping hand to keep the curls curly, hairspray was applied with wild abandon. Gossamer hair spray and VO5 came to the rescue, and we all became very adept at doing the VO5 symbol with our fingers.

For more permanent curls, there was Toni home perm solution ("Which twin has the Toni, and which has the expensive perm?") and Richard Hudnut Crème Waving Lotion. Following instructions was imperative — "Don't guess or be careless".

My brother's hair was cut by Dad until he graduated to the barber in later primary school. Dad used a hair clipper that we called Icky Ickies (don't know why) and Chris had the ultimate short back and sides. My hair was left to grow long and, apart from the occasional trim to the ends, it was only my fringe that got a regular cut. This is where sticky tape came into its own, with Mum putting it across the fringe to make sure

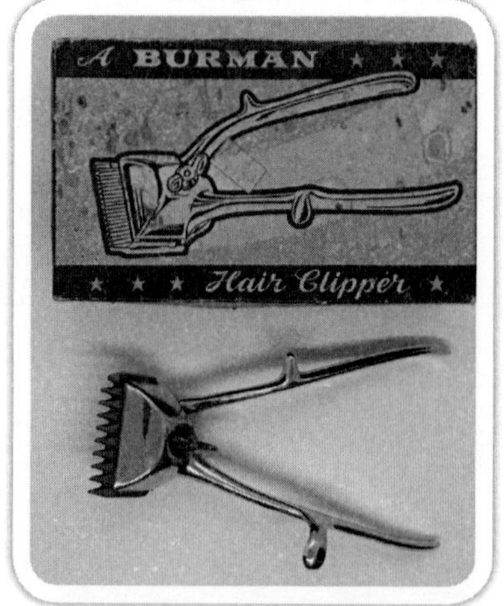

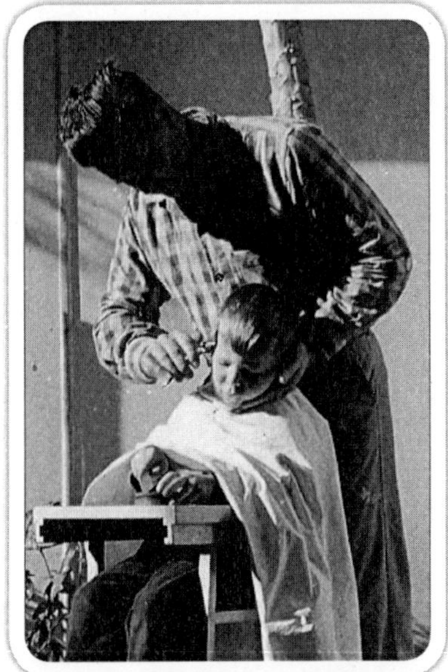

she cut it straight. The main brands were Scotch Brand, Sellotape and Durex (which unfortunately is also a brand of condom in the UK).

Horror stories of lice in long hair and the brutally archaic treatment of kerosene and head-shaving ensured that my long hair was always in plaits for school. Ribbons and home-made elastics would hold them in place. There were also the unfortunately named "doodles", which were brightly coloured string tie hair bands, and bobbles, which were an elastic loop with beads at either end to wrap around your ponytail and hold in place by catching the beads on each loop. Alice bands were used both by children and as a fashion accessory by older girls, to match their outfits and to help hold up their bouffant hairstyle.

Brylcreem had been around since the 1920s, still holding men's hair perfectly in place in its inimitable greasy way. It started to lose its popularity during the 1960s when longer, freer hair became the fashion. Brylcreem tried to claw back its market hold with ads showing girls rushing back to their Brylcreemed men, who would slyly smile and say, "I came back to Brylcreem", to which the swooning girl would reply, "And I'm glad he did".

Du Pont invented nylon and by the 1950s, toothbrushes had softer nylon bristles.

Toothpaste tubes, originally made from a tin/lead alloy (the design copied from paint tubes), were carefully wound up from the bottom to ensure the very last drop of toothpaste was squeezed out. Disaster would sometimes strike when the crushed metal would fatigue, and a little hole would allow a worm of toothpaste to escape. The tubes later transformed into plastic.

Colgate toothpaste, the first company to use a tube, would give us the "ring of confidence", while Bucky Beaver told us to "Brusha brusha brusha with the new Ipana", Nyal promised whiter teeth in 10 days and, by the way, "Are your Macleans showing?"

Fluoride toothpaste began being marketed in 1959, and while fluoride was being added to public water in various places around Australia from 1953, Brisbane would not consider the option (interestingly, Townsville began fluoridating in 1964, resulting in 45 per cent less tooth decay than Brisbane in a 1996 report).

My brother and I were given a fluoride tablet each night. They came in different pastel colours and had a slight flavour to cover up the dry texture. Whether it was this combined with regular dental check-ups or not, but I have only had three fillings in my life, and two of those were because I had braces.

Paper tissues underwent many changes from their beginnings with Kimberley-Clark's Kleenex as cold cream removers way back in the 1920s. By 1930, popular opinion was swaying towards using Kleenex tissues instead of cloth hankies as a good way to avoid the spread of germs and "the handkerchief that can be thrown away" was born. During the 1950s and 1960s, cloth hankies still seemed to be the main order of the day, with tissues kept for special occasions. Scotties tissues were a major rival for Kleenex and we were told "Don't say a tissue say a Scotties". There were coloured ones and patterned ones, and in 1967, Kleenex made space-saving purse packs and an upright box for their tissues — the Boutique box.

You could get yourself a Trim Trio at the barbers. It was a small, quasi-penknife, but aimed more at personal grooming than deeds of derring-do (although it was good for carving timber surfaces). It had three implements — a nail file with cleaning end, a bottle opener/ screwdriver and a knife blade — what more could you possibly want? They were small, fitted in your pocket really easily, and usually came with one of those ball chains to hang on your keyring. Manufactured in the States by Bassett and Co, there was usually one in most homes ... somewhere. Bassett also made other items under the Trim label such as tweezers and manicure scissors.

Dad used a cut-throat razor that he sharpened on a strop, a wide leather belt that hung on the door, frothing up shaving soap with his shaving brush in his shaving mug. He then moved on to the Gillette safety razor with the replaceable blades, screwing off the handle to pull it apart. The double-sided blades were made of carbon steel until the 1960s and rusted up, meaning you had to change the blades quite often (great for sales!). Wilkinson Sword began to sell stainless steel blades in 1965, forcing the other companies to follow suit.

It seemed a rite of passage for girls to endure the loss of a narrow strip of skin from their shins or ankles until they got used to shaving their legs with the Gillette. And didn't it bleed!!!

It wasn't until the mid-1960s that Dad got an electric shaver, a Sunbeam Shavemaster, which, as there was no power point in the bathroom, he used in the kitchen. We were fascinated with it and watched him shaving when it was new. Thank goodness he didn't give in to our requests to try it out, although he did shave the back of Chris' neck so he could feel it — I remember Mum freaking out once as she thought he had used it on my face. Electric shavers were not a cheap item, with trade-ins accepted and hire purchase available. They were packaged in presentation boxes and were a prized gift.

Shampoo was starting to be in everyone's bathroom, edging out the faithful Sunlight Soap. Originally in glass bottles, I think the move to plastic was welcomed as I am sure a number of the bottles would have hit the tiles and shattered. From memory, Blue Clinic ("Too clean for dandruff") shampoo came in a plastic bottle whose shape included a hook to hang over the curtain rail. Savlon shampoo came in a light blue, interestingly shaped squeeze bottle.

Talcum powder was thrown around with wild abandon from baby's bottoms to grown up parts. Johnson's Baby Powder, in its familiar tin, was the everyday go-to, but for special occasions there was scented talcum. Avon cleaned up pretty well here with offerings of all sorts of smells to choose from.

Originally called the Californian Perfume Company, Avon was started by a door-to-door book salesman, David McConnell, way back in 1886, who developed perfume samples that he sold alongside the books. The company was renamed Avon in 1939 and moved into Australia in 1963, offering women the opportunity to earn some money and still do what they had to in the home. The classic advertisement with "Ding dong, Avon calling" was known by everyone.

Makeup for most women consisted of face powder from a compact with a mirror, and lippy — usually a beautiful deep red. Of course, there was mascara, foundation, eye shadow, blush etc., etc., but Mum and her friends just stuck to the basics not wanting to appear too garish (and honestly, look at her, she didn't need more than that). However, the change in fashion in the 1960s, for many women, meant a heavier hand with colour and exaggerated, often fake, lashes ... that is, unless you were more of a hippy and a la naturale was the go.

Many cosmetics brands have come and gone, swallowed up or floundered in the cut-throat market, such as Lournay Cosmetics and Michel. Coles Starlet range was the budget range in the 1960s that suggested "it costs so little to look so lovely", and many girls started off their foray into makeup there as well as from the Avon catalogue pages.

Helena Rubinstein began her business in Australia selling her Crème Valaze, supposedly made with rare herbs and imported from Russia (it was actually made down the road in Flinders Lane from lanolin, wax and scent). She, Elizabeth Arden and Estee Lauder were more the David Jones end of the budget, while Revlon, Max Factor, Rimmel (Coty) and Yardley sat somewhere in the middle. Cutex stitched up the nail polish market.

Pond's Vanishing Cream and Pond's Cold Cream were the mainstay of the moisturisers for many years, with the bottle design still in use today. In fact, Mum can't really remember anything else, that is, until Oil of Ulan came on the market. It was developed in South Africa by chemist Graham Wulff for his wife. Apparently, Oil of Ulan was a play on the word lanolin, which is a key ingredient, so no, there is no such

thing as a "ulan" to extract the oil from. I always imagined it was some sort of alpaca-like animal with antelope horns. The pink, scented fluid was packaged in a heavy glass bottle with a black lid. The label had a line drawing of a lady who almost looked like a nun, in a medicinal sort of way, applying something to her face. In 1999, it became known world-wide as Ulay.

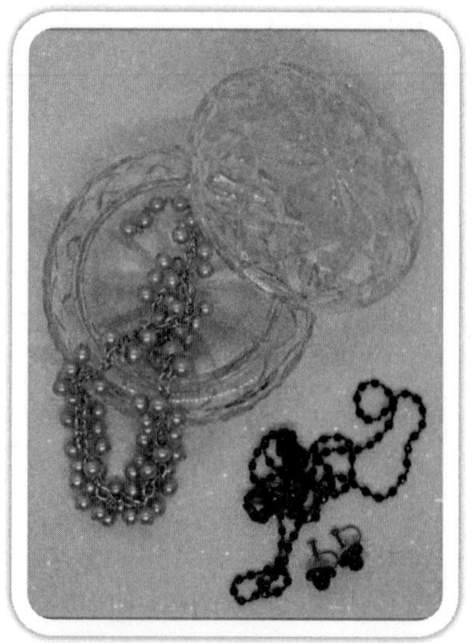

Mum's dressing table had a lovely cut crystal lidded bowl that contained secret things like tweezers, safety pins and the odd screw-backed earrings. Crystal was a big thing, and there was a vast array of items made from it that were perfect for wedding and engagement presents. Large fruit bowls, vases, napkin rings, glasses, tumblers, jugs and ashtrays — every bride of the 1950s had some crystal.

Deodorants, since their inception, were always marketed toward women with advertisements convincing them that perspiration odour ruins romance! "Make sure you are nice to be near." Yet the male deodorant market should have been so much bigger (just sayin'). Men's toiletries were sold

at the chemist giving them the slight pretence of medical association. Deodorants were known as grooming aides giving "man-sized protection" (against man-sized pong). Dad used to use a cream deodorant called Mum in a small, flat, white glass, screw top jar. Thinking back, he was quite forward thinking with this, as plenty of other blokes his age revelled in their own mystique. Maybe my Mum had a hand in this!

Other brands of the time were Odor-o-no (one of the originals from the early 20th century), Cool Charm, Arrid, Rexona and Ban. They were available in creams, sticks, roll-ons (developed from the ball point pen concept), squirt bottles, pump packs and, from the mid-1960s, in pressure pack form.

BATH ROO
PLEASE REMEMBER — DON'T FORGET —
NEVER LEAVE THE BATH ROOM WET, —
NOR LEAVE THE SOAP STILL IN THE WATER
THAT'S A THING WE NEVER OUGHT'ER.
NOR LEAVE THE TOWELS ABOUT THE FLOOR,
NOR KEEP THE BATH AN HOUR OR MORE
WHEN OTHER FOLKS ARE WANTING ONE —
PLEASE DON'T FORGET — IT ISN'T DONE !
MABEL LUCIE ATTWELL

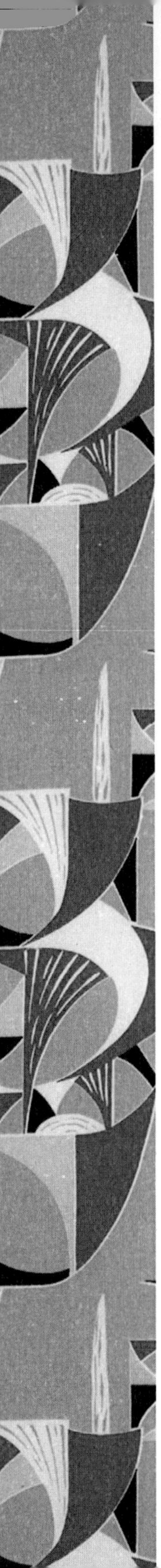

Stuff in the medicine cabinet

If we had a really awful headache or similar, Mum would crush up a Disprin ("... it's soluble aspirin") in a teaspoon and mix it with honey. They weren't given out lightly. There really wasn't anything else for kids, especially to reduce a fever, like Panadol or Nurofen as we have now.

Coughs and colds meant your chest was rubbed with Vicks Vaporub at night before you went off to sleep. Vicks was in the blue glass bottle, which unfortunately now, like everything, is just in plastic. I loved those little blue bottles. When we were really small and had stuffy noses, we would have little capsules of Karvol squeezed onto our pyjamas, which basically did the same trick, but was a gentler way of getting the fumes. Sore throats could be soothed by the man from ANTICOL.

A Eucrosol lamp was used at night-time to help allay coughs or croup. It had a strongly medicinal sort of smell, which was probably carcinogenic and is probably why there is limited information about it now. My sister-in-law and her brother were "innocently" playing with a bottle of Eucrosol when they were small children. Of course, it got spilt on their skin and they had red marks on their bodies for a very long time where it had burnt them.

Flat lemonade was the go-to for upset tummies although, as I tended to get quite a lot, the Milk of Magnesia tablets would come out. Thinking back, I probably had a bit of a lactose intolerance, but that wasn't really heard of then.

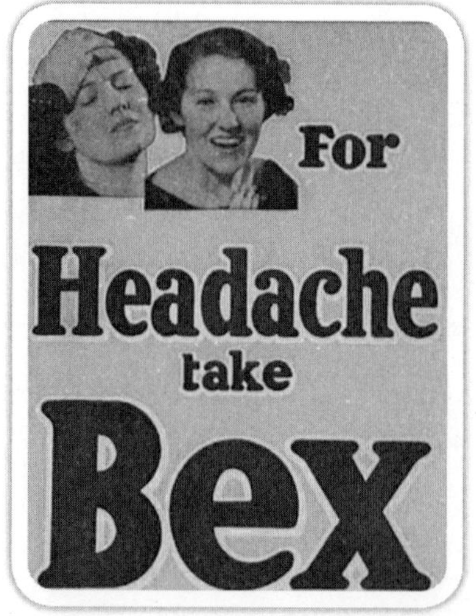

Adult-oriented (specifically women) advertisements on the trams would suggest having "a cup of tea, a Bex and a lie down". Bex was a powder compound of aspirin,

phenacetin and caffeine, which was removed from the market in 1977 due to the high incidence of related renal disease, not to mention that they were addictive. Vincent's pink powder was a similar concoction in a little paper packet and was also removed. "Take Vincents with confidence for quick three-way relief."

Yellow acriflavine and brown mercurochrome were both used for cuts and abrasions. Thankfully, Mum didn't use Dettol, which really made things sting. Savlon antiseptic cream was there for other injuries, as was Xylocaine, which contained a mild anaesthetic so was great for stings.

We also had an ancient bottle of Condy's crystals (potassium permanganate), which was useful for bacterial and fungal skin infections. If you had an ingrown toenail, you would sit with your toes suspended in a bowl of warm purple water that had some crystals dissolved in it.

Snakebite kits in those days would land you in a negligence/GBH case these days. They consisted of a small bottle of Condy's crystals, a razor blade and a bandage. You used the blade to cut across the bite, suck out the venom and blood, drop some Condy's crystals onto the puncture wound, then wrap it up with the bandage.

Hydrogen peroxide also lurked in the cupboard, which was another antiseptic, as was Fornax.

> Hydrogen Peroxide fizzed up and was great on festering sores – the more pus the bigger the fizz. Used in ears it gave a great performance. (Extract from Aniseed Balls, Billycarts and Clotheslines)

Fortunately, due to my Mum's unpleasant memories of castor oil, it never darkened our doorstep.

> In some families, children received a Friday night dose of Castor Oil to clean out the system. It certainly cleaned it out and probably all the good food consumed in the last three days as well. People were fanatical about moving their bowels, Epsom Salts and Oil of Paraffin being favourite agents. (Extract from Aniseed Balls, Billycarts and Clotheslines)

Beecham's Pills were promoted for regularity, while Ford Pills were the safe, dependable family laxative and marketed heavily as a weight loss pill that could also "help make you as attractive as the girls your husband stares at in the street".

There was the little chalice-shaped eye glass for washing out your eye to get the sand out that your brother had thrown at you.

If you couldn't get a splinter out with a flame-sterilised needle and tweezers, you could smother it with black, noxious looking drawing ointment to help remove it. It worked basically by softening the skin and letting the body do its thing of expelling whatever it was that was stuck. It was also meant to help with boils and other pussy things. Ewwwww!

Unless you were Italian, olive oil was something you bought from the chemist and warmed to dribble into ears that were aching. Mum had a beautifully shaped bottle of Fauldings Olive Oil, like a giant teardrop, in the medicine cabinet.

Mum used to put drops of Penta-Vite onto our breakfast cereal or porridge in the morning. She used to put it in the shape of a little person and call it Medicine Man. In fact, there was a stage where they were concerned that I was a bit anaemic and too skinny, so Mum would make what she called Tiger Milk in the blender, which had all sorts of good things like wheat germ, malt powder, milk, banana and Penta-Vite thrown in.

Stuff about the toilet

Not only am I old enough to have used a slate at school, but in my early years we had a dunny. It housed the regal thunderbox and stood at the end of the path that led to the garage, until the early 1960s, when sewerage was put through Mt Gravatt and we had renovations done on the house. I'm not sure if there was any subsidy for the homeowners to help with the installation of flushing toilets or not, but we ended up with a very nice addition that included a shower room (that also housed Mum's sewing area) and separate toilet.

To avoid the middle of the night trip to the toilet, we all had a chamber pot stationed under the bed. Mine was a rather pretty pink aluminum one that my grandma had given me, but was a little on the noisy side if you know what I mean. Still, at that age, I didn't really care who knew. If there was any heavy duty work to do, one would neatly place a piece of newspaper in the base of the pot.

> Chamberpots, were called pos, jerries, potties, pots, chimbos, and, most genteelly, just chambers. No wonder we as kids found it incredible to read in our storybooks of the lady who invited the charming prince into

her chamber. (Extract from Aniseed Balls, Billycarts and Clotheslines)

Of course, once flushing toilets became the mainstay in most houses, the women's magazines had to devise ways to decorate them. Enter the crocheted toilet seat cover and fitted mat with matching toilet roll cover shaped like a crinoline dress doll or other interesting concoction. New materials like nylon ribbon were used, or the fuzzy fake fur look.

Ultimately, they were all cringe worthy and, having experienced boys in the bathroom, I just don't get it.

Sorbent toilet paper, the first crepe toilet tissue in Australia, was the brand to wipe your nether regions with, and you could buy a single ply roll for the equivalent of 16 cents when it first "rolled out" in 1953. Being of a "personal nature", before self-service stores took off, you would have to buy your toilet paper from a pharmacy or newsagent, where it would be one of those under-the-counter items.

Still, it was certainly a step up from railway timetables or the green paper squares that apples came wrapped in.

> In the panstead was a pan, about 23 litres, well tarred and made of heavy grade metal. By the side of the panstead was a box containing sawdust which was put in the pan after use for absorption and covering up. This gave rise to the unfortunate name of business cakes, being given to a small pastry, generally found amongst other small cakes at parties. This consisted of a ring of puff pastry with a dollop of jam in the middle over which was sprinkled toasted coconut.
>
> Some dunnies had a small door at the back of the panstead from which the pan could be pulled out, but most had a door in the front of the panstead and people were wary of using the dunny when the dunnyman was about. He would open the door, tip a quantity of sawdust into the box, slide out the full pan, slap a tight-fitting lid on it and swing it up onto his shoulder, almost in one action, and, having slipped an empty pan into the panstead, be on his way.
>
> (Extract from Aniseed Balls, Billycarts and Clotheslines)

Those amazing nightsoil men did the job that nobody else wanted to, and they must have been incredibly strong and fit. I always remember the Hunter Brothers truck and the little swirly logo they had (vaguely like a musical treble clef on steroids).

Stuff in the bedroom

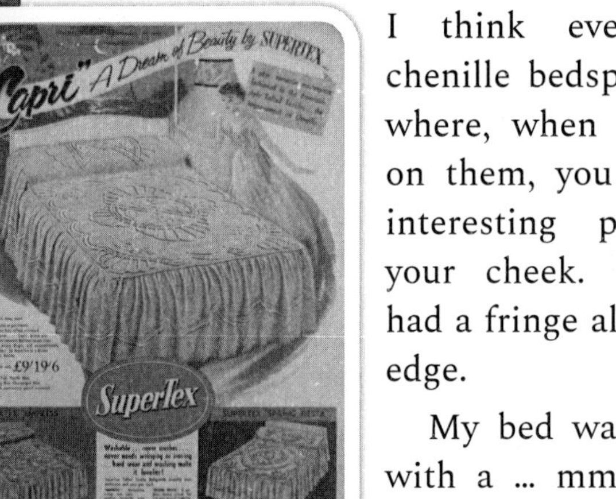

I think everyone had a chenille bedspread. The ones where, when you fell asleep on them, you woke up with interesting patterns across your cheek. Most of them had a fringe along the bottom edge.

My bed was timber frame with a ... mmmm ... how do I explain it? Something like chain mail spread across it. You could bounce on it (until Dad put wooden slats across it to stop it sagging — probably because of the bouncing). In fact, if you bounced too hard the whole metal frame would dislodge. On the back of the bedhead it said "European labour only". This was a legally required stamp put on furniture made in Australia to distinguish furniture made by Chinese workers from that made by Australians of European origin, in an early attempt to reduce the "sweat shop" conditions that existed with some Chinese manufacturers.

Before flyscreens were a done deal in houses, we had mosquito nets that were suspended from a hoop and would drape over our beds every night in summer. They were pretty effective unless one elusive mozzie snuck in as you were getting into bed, or on those really hot stinky summer nights, when they cut what little breeze there was even further.

Chances are, your blankets were made in Australia at one of the many mills of the time. The economy was still "riding on the sheep's back" in the early 1950s, with wool selling at a pound for a pound. Onkaparinga, Waverley, Physician, Warrnambool, K&K, Godfrey Hirst, Albany, Invicta, Challenge, and Castlemaine were all well-known brands, of which only a small number still survive.

We didn't have quilts or doonas then — they were called eiderdowns and were often cotton-filled (not actually eiderdown) and heavy as lead. They were padded and stitched all the way through, not like a separate quilt and cover today. Mum and Dad had a particularly flash pink sateen one.

Actil became the first company to make bed linen in Australia in 1942, making those beautiful, heavy, white, 100 per cent cotton sheets of my childhood.

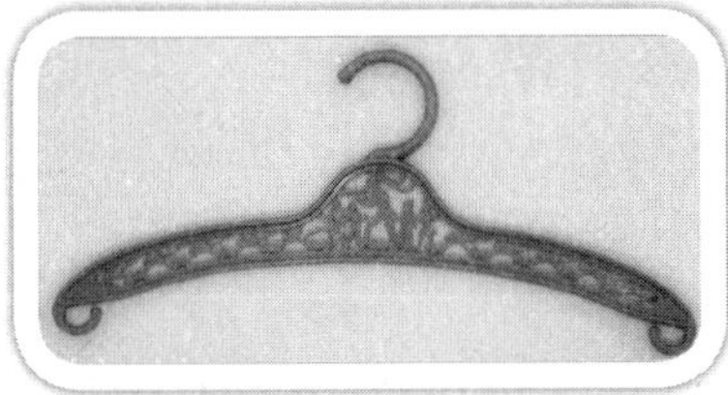

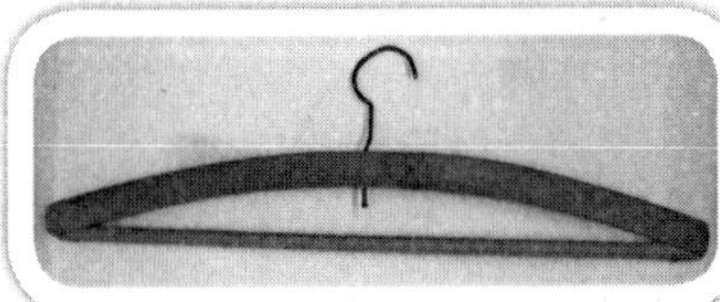

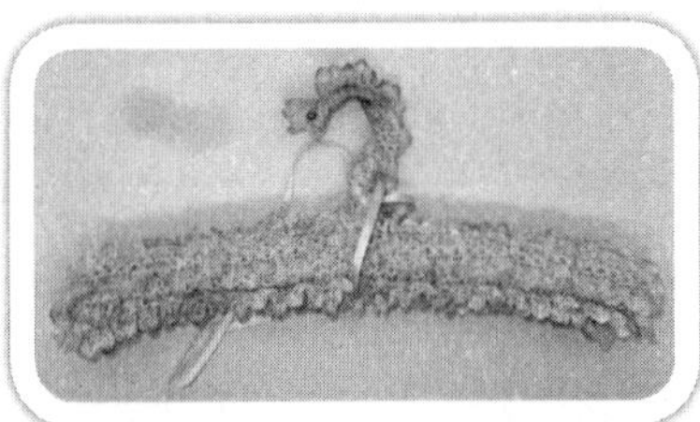

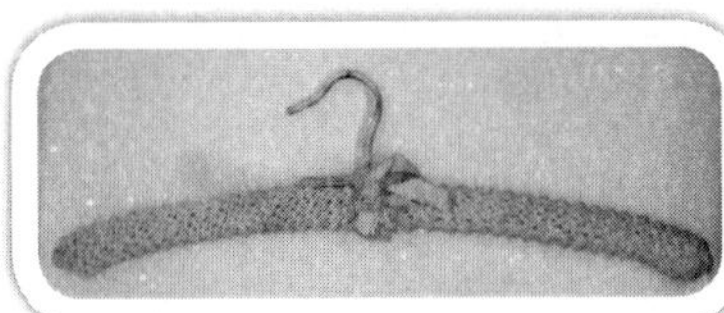

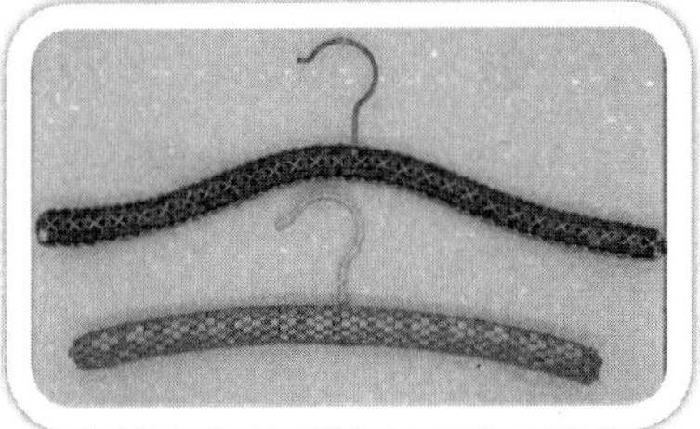

Built-in cupboards in your bedroom were virtually unheard of, so we had solid timber numbers with a couple of open shelves, four drawers and a shoe section down the bottom on one side, and then open hanging space behind the other door. And ... everything fit!! Clothes hangers varied from the cutesy, pastel-coloured, plastic baby hangers with Bambi or nursery rhyme characters on them, painted wooden ones featuring Humpty Dumpty, or knitted ones like Andy Pandy. When you grew out of those you moved onto the wire ones, or wooden ones with a wire hook.

You could get patterns for knitting, crocheting or making fabric covers for the hangers which gave them a bit of padding for more delicate items. When the nylon ribbon came in, there was always a wide assortment of styles available at the church fair. Extra special clothing had extra special frothy lacey numbers with embroidery to boot to be hung on. If you were travelling, there were some folding ones that had a plaid sort of cord covering on them.

My grandfather suffered a stroke and part of his occupational therapy was to do plastic bead work, which included coat hangers.

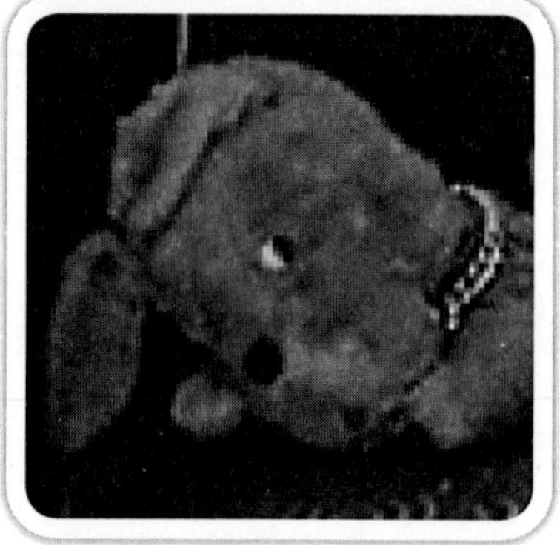

On the bed (at least on my bed) was a plethora of teddies and dolls, with barely any room for me to slide in at night. I had a pyjama dog with a zip in his tummy where I could stuff my PJs away each morning (that was the theory anyway). He ended up quite mangey-looking, with some of the straw poking out from the stitching around his neck where the metal chain rubbed. Cuddles was much loved.

Stuff we wore

The 1950s and 1960s saw great leaps in the development of synthetic fibre, although synthetics didn't really take off in Australia until the 1960s. Polyester was given different names such as Crimplene, Terylene and Dacron, while nylon surged in popularity, with the name Bri-nylon created in 1958. The big attraction of synthetic fibres was the fact they were basically wash and dry and wear again, without tedious laundering and ironing. Dad would sport a very fetching pair of crimplene shorts, long socks (held up under the fold by a garter made from sewing elastic) and Bata Kingstons when he went to work in summer, and Mum had one less thing to iron.

Dad's work shirts were often Pelaco, an Australian brand founded in Melbourne in 1913 and one of the first Australian companies to stop Saturday morning work (1908) and, in 1928, hire an industrial relations officer. By the 1950s, Pelaco employed over 1500 people in 10 factories. For more relaxed times, Penguin provided a more relaxed alternative with their collared sports shirts that had a little penguin (Pete) embroidered on the left-hand chest. It is an American icon that began in 1955. Bonds filled the casual around-the-house gap with their T-shirts.

A lot of clothes were hand-made (including the big flannelette bloomers that I wore to bed, and one day realised I had worn to school). Mum made most of our clothes with her old black electric Singer sewing machine, carefully drafting, on the kitchen table, the patterns from the Enid Gilchrist pattern books or using premade patterns. Big sheets of brown paper that packages had been wrapped in at Bayards (and tied up with string), or similar, were carefully flattened and stored for these drafting episodes. David Jones paper wasn't as good as it had hounds tooth pattern on one side, which was distracting. There was even a book for doll's

clothes from which she made many clothes for my Barbie doll.

Stockings were still held up by a garter belt, with the all-in-one pantyhose not hitting the shelves until the early 1960s. Of course, the mini skirt really helped rocket those sales. It seems funny now that the garter belt and stockings are something you might find in Honey Birdette windows rather than the everyday item that everyone wore. Mind you, Honey Birdette's version are probably not what one would have worn to a Ladies' Guild meeting.

I had my very first pair of sneakers in kindy. They were a green tartan pair and I thought I was very cool sneaking up on my hapless teacher. They were accompanied by my Robin My-T-Tuff socks, and both they and I graduated into Bata Ponytails when I went to Grade One, while Dad was "a man of action" in his Bata Kingstons for work.

These, of course, were religiously cleaned to a mirror shine each morning with Kiwi or Nugget boot polish. Kiwi shoe polish was actually an Australian invention. Developed in 1906 by William Ramsay, he called it Kiwi in honour of his wife's country of birth. Kiwi shoe polish was different to the competition in that it also restored colour, preserved the leather and helped with its water resistance. Kiwi went on to international fame, especially after it was used extensively during World War I by both American and British armies to help with the water-resistance for their boots in the horrendous conditions in the trenches.

Any self-respecting woman (or her daughter) would wear a rubber bathing cap if you went for a swim. They weren't the slick silicon things of today, but glorious fabrications with flowers, swirls and twirls all over them in an array of colours. We stuck with the basic model, a sort of bubbly rubber number. I can sort of understand wanting to keep hair out of the pool filter, but wearing it in the ocean was really a waste of time — my hair still got wet, sandy and salty, and it usually came off on my second trip in on the rubber surf mat.

My swimmers, or togs as we called them, were made from a textured, polyester knit that took a while to dry. The bikini was starting to appear, although was still considered a little risqué and certainly not appropriate for one as young as I. Scandalously, in 1962, Ursula Andress, in *Dr No*, strode from the water wearing nothing but a knife and bikini. Australia was faster to accept this form of swimwear than the Americans, who still held the trophy for being prudes.

Men wore high-waisted pants known as swimming trunks made from polyester knit, nylon or gaberdine. When surfing later became popular, many wore board shorts, whether or not they had a board. Speedos in gleaming satin lastex (rather larger than today's version) were mainly for those involved in water sports or for surf lifesavers. Many men's swimmers had a sort of fabric panel across the front (half skirt trunk they were called), something like a wall to cover anything that might hint there was more there than what a Ken doll might have.

Cat's-eye glasses, originally called Harlequin glasses back in the 1930s, were already popular in 1950, and were first designed for prescription lenses. Lots of my friends' mums wore them as did some of our teachers, but I always thought they looked a bit severe. Audrey Hepburn's cat's-eye sunglasses in *Breakfast at Tiffany's* in 1961 set the sunglass trend.

Dressing gowns for men were a definite! Onkaparinga made woollen dressing gowns with enormous pockets in the familiar plaid pattern with a corded tie that had tassels. They were a little prickly, but both my Dad and brother had one and they were really warm.

Woollen jumpers (or cardigans and pullovers) were often homemade, with Mum slaving over a pair of hot needles for nights on end following intricate patterns of different stitches from the Paton's or Coat's books. They were usually incredibly warm and could be incredibly heavy unless she chose to use a smaller ply. Windcheaters with a zip-up front and pockets were also popular, and were made from a fleecey lined cotton fabric.

In 1958, Hungarian immigrants Alice and Louis Kennedy started their Glomesh factory in Bondi, creating must-have fashion items in the classic gold, silver and enamel mesh. They moved into a variety of items including compacts, lipstick holders, cigarette cases, atomisers and glasses cases.

Gloves and hats were an expected part of a woman's apparel if you were going out or to church. White or cream were the favourite colours and beautifully clean gloves were the mark of a lady. They were also good to cover up gardening and washing-up hands, which according to advertisements could completely ruin a lady's reputation. Hats were a strange concoction of pill boxes, sometimes with veiling in the front, cloches, straw hats and some that just looked like a cow pat.

It was often the older generation who stuck with these as everyday traditions, and they gradually faded out. You would still often see men wearing the old felt trilby around town, particularly older men, who would still tip their hat to a lady.

The Blue Bird of Happiness was a common theme for little ones, and gifts for baby often included a gold bracelet with an enamelled blue bird on the locket, or a brooch with safety chain for older girls.

We were a Bond's family, with the boys sporting the Chesty Bond athletic singlets and high waist sports briefs with the green lines around the waist band, while we girls also stuck with the white wonders (read BIG white undies), Cotton Tops singlets and the more refined ladies singlet with the thinner shoulder strap. Cottontails were first produced in 1955 using yards of fabric until the bikini brief was available in 1966. George Bond grew some of Australia's first ever cotton in the late 1920s, opening the first ever Australian cotton spinning mill in Wentworthville in the early 1930s.

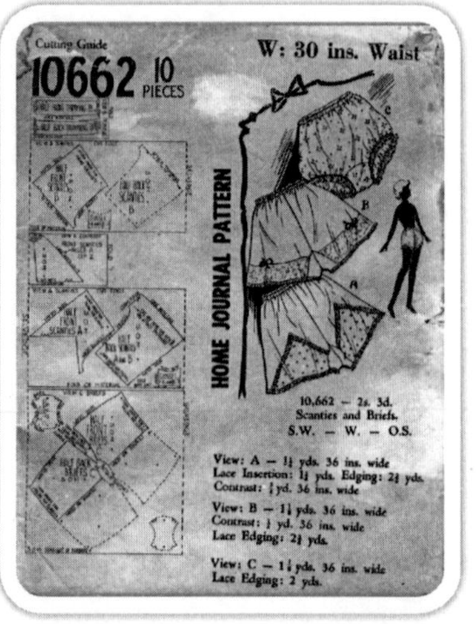

Prior to Cottontails, Mum's underwear was high waisted, elasticised waist and legs — undies made from fabric like Milanese, which was a very fine knitted fabric with a diamond-like pattern on one side and vertical rib on the other. They were called 'briefs' — go figure! It was lightweight, smooth and resistant to runs. There was the French knicker as well, which was a more open leg variety.

Petticoats, slips, panty girdles, longline bras, singlets and camisoles all abound in women's advertising. It's a wonder they could move at all with all the undergarments they were meant to wear. After the austerity of the war years, femininity was back, and underwear was once again pretty and lacy (except the white wonders).

Stuff we played with

I know I could fill chapters with toys that kids played with in these two decades, so I will just go with what our family and friends knew.

Richard Knerr and Arthur Melin of the Wham-O Company created what became a huge international fad — the hula-hoop. While Australian children had been twirling bamboo hoops around their waists as part of their school sport, these two Americans saw a marketing opportunity to make brightly coloured plastic versions. I had a blue one.

Flinging pie tins from The Frisbie Baking Company in Connecticut was a fun thing at Ivy League colleges like Yale. These same guys renamed it the Frisbie and the sixties did the rest.

The game of Mr Potato Head, devised in 1952 by George Lerner of New York, originally consisted of just pieces, using a real potato for the body. Maybe if it had been developed by a mum, the head would have been part of the original plastic design, knowing that kids would leave the potato to putrefy!

My brother had a red metal pedal car when he was small, which we called the "bomb car". From this he moved on to a large blue tricycle that had a ledge at the back that I could stand on. Scooters followed one Christmas (red this time), mine was a bit smaller than Chris', with smaller wheels. Of course, as he outgrew his, it came to me. Cyclops was originally an Australian manufacturer of metal toys including pedal cars, tricycles, scooters and wagons.

My wooden rocking horse, on which I had many enjoyable rides, wasn't a fancy one, just a painted one on rockers but I loved it.

We had a set of metal stilts that we wobbled around the back patio on, suggesting friends have a go whenever they came over.

With the popularity of some of the tamer Western TV shows, cowboys and "Injuns" became a great game outside. I even had the complete Annie Oakley outfit with guns and Chris had the Roy Rogers set.

Of course, we had absolutely no idea of the historical significance of

any of it, just like the war games that the boys played with their little green plastic soldiers, which came in about five different poses to hold a plethora of weapons including rifles, machine guns, pistols, grenades and bazookas. You could even get jeeps and tanks. There were also “enemy” soldiers available, with the German soldiers being a dull kind of grey while the Japanese came in yellow (what else?). My parents’ generation had only just come out of World War II, so it was still all in their recent memory.

There were, of course, war comics to feed the blood lust, and from them we learned a smattering of German and thought that all Japanese soldiers had buck teeth and glasses.

Dad made a fort for Chris for his 10th birthday, complete with crenellated walls and towers and match-firing cannon, while I had an enormous (seemed like it to me then) doll’s house that my cousins had handed down to me. It was all on one level but had a fireplace, which I thought was really special as they were a rarity in Brisbane households.

We played Old Maid, Fish, and Happy Families with Dickie Dose and his evil-looking mother. There was the Magic Slate with its peel off acetate sheet, supposedly used during the 1960s in the American Embassy in Russia to circumvent supposed listening devices. The precursor to this toy was one where there was a sheet of glass that you drew on with pencil, and then rubbed it out.

The famous trolls with soft fuzzy hair were designed by a Danish woodcutter in 1959. They were cute and crazy, and we all wanted one (or two or three) to stick on the ends of our pencils. No wonder they had that surprised look!

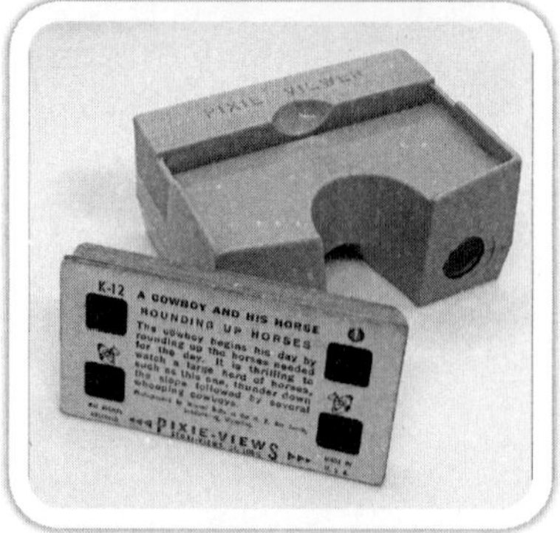

View-Master reels brought pictures to life with their 14 transparencies in seven pairs. This made seven stereoscopic images producing a binocular view. Disney scenes or travel views were popular items. We had the Pixie Viewer, which had four images on a card.

Spirographs helped us to draw amazing patterns, while the metal push-down spinning top kept us amused for ages.

Slot car racing kits like Scalextrics had the boys fixated, as did the Hornby train sets. Of course, Hornby kept adding to their collection, keeping pocket money going in one direction.

Meccano kept budding engineers busy for hours. We had a plastic version of something similar (for much younger engineers) with orange nuts and bolts.

Matchbox cars came about when Jack O'Dell, a partner in Lesney Products, decided he needed to make a toy for his daughter that she could take to school, the school rule being that toys could not come to school unless they could fit in a matchbox.

The rest is history, as they say. Dinky toys were already around at this stage, being manufactured by Meccano, and they became rivals in the sandpits and backyards of the world.

A cotton reel with four nails in the top was used to perform French knitting, making copiously long tubes for no particular purpose.

Skipping ropes ranged from random pieces of light rope to wooden handled ones with stripes painted around the edge of each handle. Long hemp ropes were nicked from the shed so you could do group skipping. There were numerous games and chants we said, usually including something about a boyfriend, or ones that quickly changed the rhyming word to something more dignified.

Suzie had a steamboat
The steamboat had a bell
Suzie went to Heaven
The steamboat went to..
Hello operator, give me number nine
If you disconnect me
I'll kick your big ...
Behind the fridgerator
There was a piece of glass
Suzie went and sat on it
And cut her little ...
Ask me no more questions

I'll tell you no more lies

The cows are in the meadow

Making apple pies, PIES, PIES, PIES

(this is the pepper part 'til you tripped up)

The traditional chants must have been passed on from the distant past.

Bread and butter, marmalade jam

Tell me the name of your young man. The number of peppers you could do revealed the initials while ...

When are you going to be married? Similarly disclosed the name of the month.

The question of ...

What are you going to your wedding in? had the choices of coach, carriage, sulky, buggy, motor car, truck and it was critical not to go out at this point because the next option was dunnycart.

The experts of fast skipping were put through their paces with the chant of *Salt, Mustard, Vinegar, Pepper*! The last word being the signal for the high speed turning of the rope. (Extract from Aniseed Balls, Billycarts and Clotheslines)

We also raided Mum's sewing cabinet to get a nice long piece of elastic to play elastic fantastic, once again with boyfriend-oriented chants as we went through the routine.

Cat's Cradle, thought to be one of the oldest games in the world and played in various nations, used a loop of wool that you intertwined through your fingers to make different shapes.

Knuckles, another old game, progressed from carefully saving the knuckle bones from the weekend roasts 'til you had five, to being able to buy brightly coloured plastic ones.

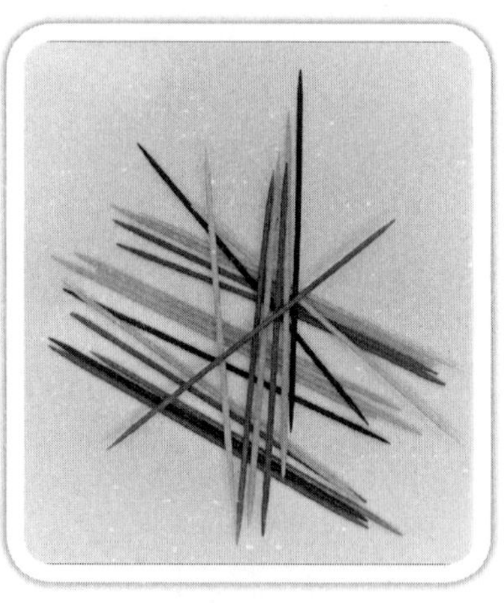

We had the Coca Cola Yo-yo International Professional Team visit us at school, which was awesome! The first Coca Cola yo-yo came to Australia in 1958, but it wasn't until 1960 that Australia really embraced the Coke promotion when they introduced competitions. This is probably one of the only school parades that I remember. They were so unbelievably cool and could do amazing things with their yo-yos, and we all wanted to grow up and be yo-yo professionals.

We all tried to convince our parents that we needed one and so the profit margins of Coca Cola continued to grow. Everyone practised their moves with walking the dog, around the world and rock the cradle. The moves were not without danger,

and often an around the world trip would end up with a split lip, or worse, if the length wasn't judged properly.

There was Mousetrap, Ker Plunk, dominoes, Chinese checkers, Sorry, marbles, Sketch-a-graph, Monopoly, Scrabble, Snakes and Ladders, Tiddly Winks, Pick up Sticks, Concentration, Cluedo, not to mention draughts and chess. Twister originally appeared in 1966, but was whisked away briefly as it was considered a bit risqué.

Marbles would suddenly appear. The game was a serious one with strict rules. The marbles themselves came in a great variety and all were named. There were Glassies, Agates, Stars, Commons, Stickers, Ballies (large steell ball bearings), Alleys, Blood Alleys, Stoneys, Tors and Clay Stonkers as well as Eye Droppers which were very large. If you played for keeps you had to state this loudly, preferably before witnesses, before you began the game. (Extract from Aniseed Balls, Billycarts and Clotheslines)

We would spend wet days colouring in or using rubber stamps to decorate pages. There were cut-out doll's clothes that you could dress up a paper doll with, folding over the little tabs so it would hang on the doll. Some of these were even already scored so you could easily push the pieces out.

Dolls came in all shapes and sizes, and materials from cloth to hard plastic, vinyl and celluloid. I think every girl ended up with a kewpie doll on a stick from the Show. Barbie, developed by Ruth Handler of Mattel fame and named after her daughter Barbara, was "born" on 9 March 1959. She arrived wearing a black and white zebra-striped bathing suit, sandals, sunglasses and gold hoops in her ears. It wasn't until 1965 that the poor love was able to bend her legs.

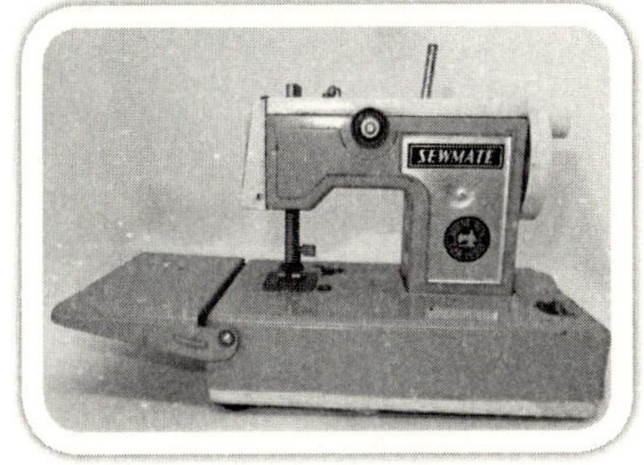

I had a pink plastic tea set that had a very French poodle transfer on each piece and lacy edge to the plates. It even had a tall coffee pot. Much Milo was made up in that and "shared" with my special clique of dolls and teddies. Girls would often get the mini ironing board and iron, mini sewing machine and mini everything else to make them just like Mum. I even had a little dustpan and brush set called "Mummy's Little Help", which is quite different to the ones mentioned later in the book!

One of Mum's old hatboxes was filled with the most fantastic dressing up items, which included everything from old bridesmaid dresses to pirate outfits. I would often wander down the road to visit our lovely old neighbour wearing a satin petticoat, gloves, copious necklaces and clunky sandals. Mum had the Enid Gilchrist costume book, from which she made some brilliant dress-ups like Robin Hood and caped crusaders.

Kids' annuals were a big thing, and were either related to specific characters like Sooty and Sweep, Rin Tin Tin or Noddy and Big Ears (even though he was feeling a little queer ... and then got banned because of it), or were more a collection of stories, games and activities.

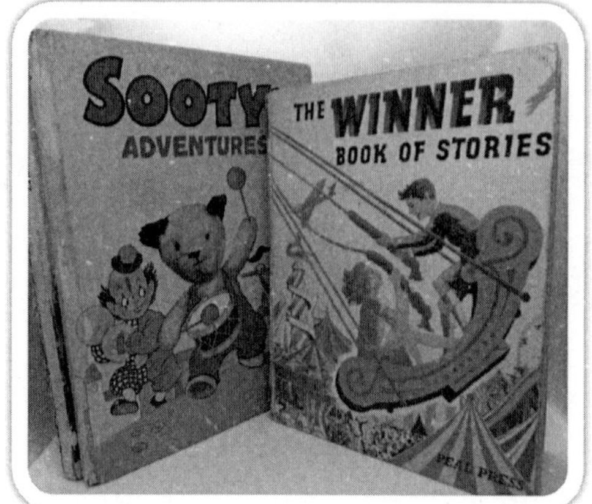

Comics were a big part of growing up, from funny cartoons like Tom and Jerry, to the more "serious" cowboys and Indians, and war comics mentioned previously. At the end of the comics were always ads for ant farms or the classic Sea Monsters (which were basically brine shrimp) that had castles and little crowns and things ... no, seriously, they did!

Ladybird Books and Little Golden Books were probably on everyone's shelves with a plethora of titles to choose from. Ladybird Books were probably more in the educationally oriented line, while Little Golden Books were just nice stories and included Disney tales and images from the movies. I love the recent spoof of Ladybird

Books with adult versions of the stories and their classic picture style.

In 1957, Dr Seuss published *How the Grinch Stole Christmas* and his classic *The Cat in the Hat*, for which he is probably best known. This latter book was written in response to an article about the low levels of children's reading. He was asked to write a book using a small number of words, and it was so successful, he continued to write in this style. *One Fish, Two Fish, Red Fish, Blue Fish,* published in 1960, was my first Dr Seuss book, the same year that *Green Eggs and Ham* came out.

Dad and Chris played tennis with their old wooden racquets that were kept in racquet presses to prevent them from warping. Racquets were first made of laminated wood in 1947, but it wasn't until 1968 that they started making them in steel.

Kids were into collecting things, whether it was stamps, coins, rocks or bits of used chewing gum. My brother had an insect collection full of poor, chloroformed butterflies and shiny beetles, each scientifically named and mounted.

Naturally, having an enquiring mind, he couldn't work out how the chloroform worked so took a big sniff himself.

My collecting foray was with shells, and once again, they were all scientifically named and sorted. I was the youngest member of the Brisbane branch of the Malacological Society (I guess I was a bit nerdy) and entered my shells into competitions, even winning shell of the show once for my beautiful wentletrap.

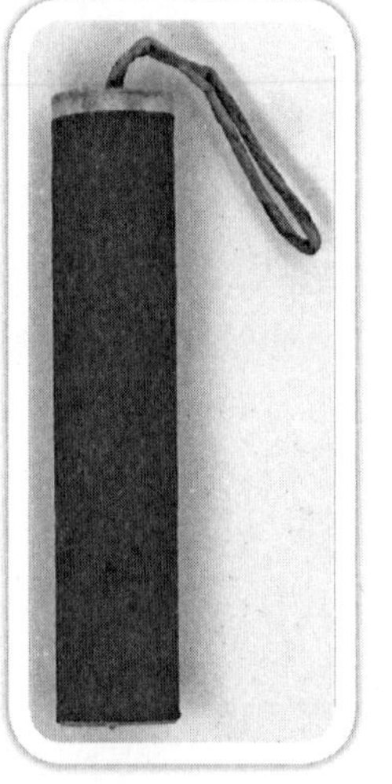

Mum and Dad supported us wholeheartedly with our collecting, encouraging both of our scientific endeavours, quietly smiling when people would give me a couple of broken, worm-eaten shells "for my collection" along with a pat on the head.

Crackers are a revered memory for many, and were all available, for a glorious but short time, like lollies in a glass-topped counter at the corner store.

There were throwdowns (dirt with a cap in them that exploded when you threw them hard at the ground). Tom Thumbs were all tied together in rows — they were available in a block of about 10 sheets (if you were incredibly rich) or you could buy one sheet.

It was considered a terrible waste to let them all go off at once, so they would be painstakingly untied so you ended up with individual crackers. If you were game enough, you would hold one right at the end and light it. They usually blew out the side, but on very rare occasions they would blow backwards — bit like a game of Russian roulette on a less permanent (but still painful) scale. If your Tom Thumb didn't have a wick or it had come out, you would break them in half and light the broken part which would go *sizzzz* — and surprisingly they were called sizzers!

Skyrockets were used to shoot up the drain pipe that led from a house to the gutter. Occasionally, you would get a result and see smoke come out of the pipe on their roof. Penny skyrockets were often thrown to give them more lift. If you threw them too quickly, they would come down back at you before they exploded at height. Never sure just where they were heading, you just ran.

Double bungers were highly prized, not just because they made a loud noise — they could be used for all sorts of inspirational purposes.

Jumping jacks were unpredictable as they went off jumping around on the ground. To save on matches, you always used a piece of mozzie coil to light your crackers.

Cracker night was fiendishly exciting, and was a way for fathers to legitimately feed their residual childhood pyromania, setting up Roman candles, Catherine wheels and all manner of rockets and noisy explosions. Today the smell of the fireworks at fetes and festivals brings back wonderful memories.

Crackers were banned in Queensland in 1972, mainly due to excessive injuries, including the third largest reason for eye injury at that time ... who would have guessed?

Stuff we had outside

As cars became more popular, yards had to include a garage or shed, as we called ours. Our shed was made of fibro with big heavy double doors that opened out. At one end was Dad's work area with his heavy-duty work bench and vice, while on the wall behind it was a board with hooks and outlines for his hand tools. Hand drill, hand saws, screwdrivers, hand-turned grinding wheel, brace and bit — all beautifully made tools that he looked after in his inimitable way. Once done with all his dirty work, he would wash the grime away with a cake of good old Solvol. Solvol has been around for more than 100 years using the combination of citrus oils and pumice ("Whatever you're into, Solvol gets it out!").

Electric tools were in use in industry, but domestic versions weren't so common and were expensive. Black and Decker started manufacturing in Australia in 1956 in Victoria, still with metal casings. Bosch later created the first power tool with a plastic casing — significantly safer when using 240 volt power! (Interestingly, it was an Australian, Arthur Arnot, who, in 1889, took out a patent on the world's first electric drill.)

With the large house blocks, mowing the lawns was a regular job, especially in summer. We had a Qualcast push mower with metal wheels and a wooden handle. This was superseded by a blue Pope that had a metal handle, orange hubcaps and rubber tyres. It had a catcher on the back that Dad would empty out on the garden or in the compost area.

Being a bit of a perfectionist, Dad would mow, rake and then mow again to catch those sneaky blades that had hidden the first go over.

A revelation in grass management came about in the 1950s when Mervyn Victor Richardson from Concord in NSW invented the Victa lawnmower in 1952. Using a Villier's two-stroke engine, with a peach tin

for a fuel tank, he developed a smaller, cheaper and much lighter version of the existing rotary mower. By the following year, demand for the mowers had become enough for Richardson to manage full-time the new Victa Mowers company. Eight million lawnmowers have been sold in over 30 countries since then. After a couple of ownership changes, Briggs and Stratton purchased the company in 2008. Along with the Hills Hoist, the Victa lawnmower is another iconic Australian invention. Dad had his Victa mower right up until the 1980s when he finally had to "let it go".

To trim up the edges he had a metal lawn edger with a circular blade and a little metal step to push your foot down on to cut the grass as it rolled along.

Dad was a great gardener, developing a forest with rockeries, birdbaths, camping area and pendulous staghorns up the back, and vegetable and flower gardens around the yard. Of course, to make sure things stayed hunky dory in the garden, there were the bug sprays, dusting powders, fertilisers and other not so nice chemicals that were completely accepted as good for the garden and good for you. The garden hose had brass screw-on fittings at either end — none of this snap-on stuff. Whenever I smell water on hot concrete, I am transported back to hot summer days, having a hose "swim" in the backyard, my brother and I in our togs and yes, I had my bathing cap on.

Popular flowers of the time were the blue hydrangea, orange browallia, blue plumbago, orange crucifix orchids (everyone had that one length of garden that was dry and full of succulents like mother-in-law's tongue, mother of millions and crucifixes), blue-centred African daisies, purple bachelor's buttons, dahlias, brunsfelsias (yesterday, today and tomorrow) and azaleas.

Mum would often arrange flowers at church and used a lot of different plants from our garden, including climbing pothos and other greenery, as well as that hot favourite in the vase stakes, gladioli. The vase would have a spikey weighted "stayput" in

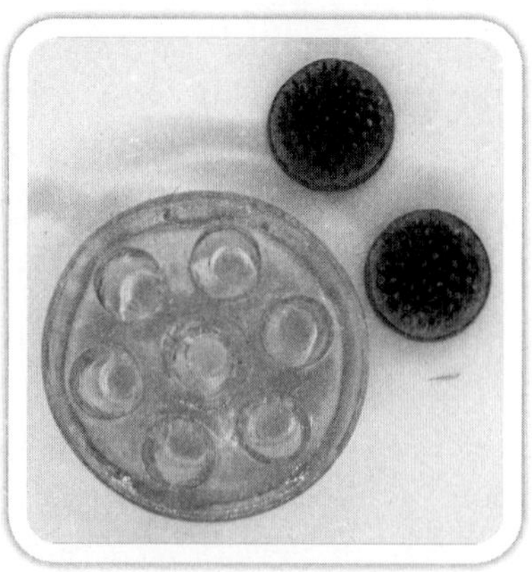

the bottom or a "frog" in the neck to keep the flowers in place.

Dad built us a sandpit underneath the house between some of the concrete posts. Here we would spend many hours playing with our buckets, spades, Matchbox and Dinky cars, being careful to cover it up again at night to stop neighbourhood cats doing what they do in sand.

Climbing trees was a great pastime, and my friend Helen had the best mulberry tree in her backyard. In spring we would gorge ourselves on its richly purple fruit. Its branches spread out over the neighbour's garage, and interestingly, the roof had a few small holes in it that we could peer through and see their white car. Even more interestingly, mulberries would just fit through the hole.

If there was a tree in the yard, or an accessible joist under the house, there would be a swing attached to it. Usually just a plank of wood with a hole either end to thread some rope through. Hills made swing sets for the more upwardly mobile, which usually included a couple of rings on chains, a chain swing and a long swing where two people could sit either end. Horrendous dentally oriented stories abound of course from this last special item. We would swing so high on these that the swing set would rock from side to side.

Chris and I also made good use of a small corrugated water tank that we would sit in and roll down our grass ramp, using the fence at the bottom to stop us.

Boys had their own set of outdoor equipment and pursuits. A helpful sign to wildlife would have been, "Abandon hope all ye who enter this yard", as anything that moved was fair game. Lizards of all types, from the humble skink to the more exotic bearded dragon, were highly prized either to keep as pets or attached to skyrockets and renamed Yuri.

Slingshots, gings or shanghais were potentially lethal weapons, but boy, weren't they fun? They were usually lovingly homemade from a forked stick or piece of heavy wire, with rubber bike tubing tied between the forks. Thoughts are that the term "shanghai" came from the old English word "shangie" for cleft stick, whereas "ging" might simply be the sound it makes when fired.

Go-carts were another outdoor pursuit, with interesting constructions made from old wooden fruit boxes, wheels nicked from an old pram and rope hooked through the pivoting front axle. Brakes relied on thick soled shoes. Much skin would be lost in endeavours down hills and around corners, but it was all good fun (... until someone loses an eye). Dad always stressed that these were not billy carts — billy carts were pulled along by billy goats!

Concrete statues in the garden seemed to be more prolific in suburbs where there were more Italians. They loved their gardens and loved to decorate them. There was one place we always drove past that had chooks on verandah railings, gnomes, kangaroos that sat on their haunches watching the passing traffic, deer that posed as if stunned in the headlights, an Aboriginal holding his woomera and spear, with the foot of one leg permanently attached to the knee of the other, and Manneken Pis filling up a bowl in his own special way.

Stuff we had in the car

When Mum fell pregnant in 1956, Dad decided he needed to trade up the BSA motorbike for a car and bought a cream FJ. I have vague memories of red seats and, in the boot, we had a latchhook rug of a tiger that my uncle made.

In 1964, Dad bought another Holden, this time a brown EH station wagon with the number plate NUN 848 (I know — some things just stick with you!). I think it was a combination of growing children and not enough room for camping equipment that inspired the purchase. Mum made brown-checked curtains for the back for when we slept in the car.

The back of the car had the split window with top half opening up and the bottom half opening out, making an extension of the floor. Station wagons were awesome for going to the drive-in movies. You could lie in the back and watch (or fall asleep when you were little). I do remember my friend Julie's Dad had a Holden Special, where the back window wound down. It was great sitting in the back as they drove along with the window down, no doubt sucking in a share of carbon monoxide.

Kids were often thrown into the back of the station wagon for trips, and I well remember falling asleep in the back on the way home from my Gran's at Auchenflower, watching the stars and the lights on the buildings as we drove through Brisbane. I distinctly remember the chook on top of Redcomb House in town that used to peck up and down.

Dad had also made a timber trailer (which my brother still has) that we used for our holiday trips. He first painted it cream to match the FJ and then painted it brown to match the EH.

When they bought a Franklin Skyline fibreglass caravan in 1965, Dad repainted the red stripe in brown to also match. Mum made curtains and added bobbles on the bottom edge. He kept the cute, 14 foot, egg-shaped caravan in immaculate condition, and I remember him repainting the inside, warming up the tins of enamel paint so it didn't leave streaks when you brushed it on. The van ran on both 12 V (plugged into the car battery) and 240 V.

There was a gas fridge and cooker and, initially, my brother and I slept on the table, which folded down into a double bed at the front of the van. Dad was still towing that van around when he was 77. It is now off the road and resides under cover at our place — still much loved.

The annexe, which came a bit later, gave us all more room. Chris and I had heavy hessian army stretchers that squeaked when you rolled over in your kapok sleeping bag. Mum made liners for our sleeping bags to keep them cleaner, which was a great idea but a rarity.

I was always so disappointed that, because we had a station wagon, we couldn't have a dog on the back shelf with a bobbing head. Of course, I am not sure even if we'd had a sedan whether Mum's reason would have stood for anything.

Front seatbelts were mandatory in all new cars in Australia from 1 January 1969, although anchor points were required from 1964. Dad had seatbelts installed in the back when he bought the EH, and many friends had to be shown how to use them. In fact, Victoria, in 1970, was the first in the "Western world" to legislate for compulsory wearing of seatbelts. Queensland followed in 1972. Just something we take for granted now.

The EH had the old batwing air vents in the front, which were a help when it rained so there was still a bit of air inside. These vents could also be inverted right around to allow a big gush of air inside, which was especially good when our dog Bobby had thrown up in the back. We also had a window shield on the front driver's side window, which also helped keep the rain out and the air flowing.

To protect the windscreen on our road trip holidays towing the caravan, there was a stone shield which was made from plastic, with suction cups in each corner. It probably wouldn't make standard requirements now and actually did get blown off once when it was parked, and the wind was howling from behind. Considering the roads back then and the places we ventured, it was probably a good investment.

A foot-operated dip switch for the lights was on the floor, and the gears were the classic three in the tree.

Stuff we had on holidays and picnics

The Esky Auto Box (the Esky brand wasn't registered until 1961) had a metal inner and outer lining with a layer of cork sheet as insulation, and was designed with a triple level food section and space to carry six one pint bottles. We now tend to call any insulated container an esky.

Shell Road Guides were published by the Shell Touring Service of the Shell Oil Company of Australia Ltd. There were guides for pretty much the whole of Australia, providing not only the maps but information about road surfaces, distances between places, and, most importantly, where the Shell service stations were. In a time before the 24 hour 7 day a week petrol station, you had to watch the gauge and plan ahead. There were listings in the paper of which stations were on

roster and would be open over the weekends just in case.

Shell even had passports for the kids, which they could have stamped with an image relevant to the area of the service station they were stopping at.

Another clever marketing ploy by Shell was the Shell Project Cards and book to put them in.

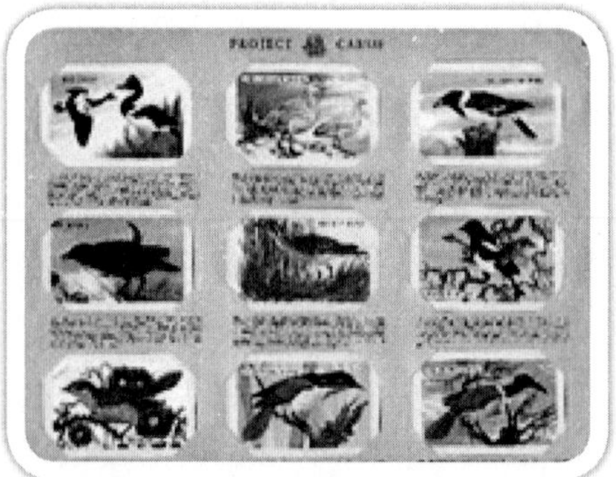

This ensured the kids would hassle you to get your petrol at Shell ("Go well, go Shell") and bypass Golden Fleece (gone to Caltex in 1989) and Amoco ("the nice clean petrol" that merged with BP in 1998). Tony the Tiger helped "put a tiger in your tank" at Esso. So popular was he that people attached a fake tiger's tail to their exhaust or one coming out of their petrol tank. Esso was acquired by Mobil in 1990. Total ("oooh what a gas") went to Ampol in 1982, which then merged with Caltex in 1995. In those good old days, you could sit in your car while the attendant filled your tank, cleaned your windscreen and checked your oil.

Our Fire-King peach lustre mugs were our designated camping or picnic cups, and still bring back memories of hot tea in the morning underneath the green-roofed canvas tent.

A vacuum flask was imperative if you wanted to stop on the way for a cuppa. Thermos, although originally a brand name, ended up being the generic term for these useful picnic items with the glass inner. Stanley, whose flasks are made from metal, also use the term thermos, but have to use the lower case to differentiate it from the original.

If you were a blue-collar worker, or helping a mate build a shed, you tended to use the Stanley thermos, as it was pretty well indestructible on the worksite. For some reason, plaids seemed to be the theme for picnics, with blankets, cloths and bags flaunting tartans of one clan or another. Thermos followed suit with their flasks.

Before the disposable culture took over, plastic or melamine plates were used for picnics or camping, and of course, all were taken home and washed for re-use.

We had one of those multi-coloured beach umbrellas that dotted the sands at the coast each holiday.

Sunscreen, other than Pinke Zinc, wasn't really heard of, although Dad had a special compounded mix from the chemist that we put on our faces. I think it was heavily composed of zinc but had a great holiday smell (to me anyway). The rest of our bodies weren't covered or smeared in anything, and we did get sunburned, although Mum and Dad were careful with the amount of sun we got and tried to keep us under cover when they could.

Coppertone began producing its suntan lotion in the 1940s, although its cute little, pale-bottomed model didn't appear until 1956. It combined the "sun tanning properties of cocoa butter with the skin conditioning qualities of lanolin blocking out the harmful burning rays and admitting the sun tanning rays". Piz Buin came out around the same time as Coppertone and was named after Mt Piz Buin, where the developer had earlier got badly sunburned.

Stuff we had at school

From 1952, Queensland primary schools had eight grades, after which students went to secondary school where there were four year levels — sub-junior, junior, sub-senior and senior. In the early 1960s, Grade 8 moved to secondary school.

During the 1950s, school uniforms were a hit and miss affair, with most children at Mt Gravatt State School wearing plain clothes, accompanied by the occasional shoes, although many were dumped in bags on the way to school. By the 1960s, Mt Gravatt State School had a full uniform for boys and girls in the flattering colours of grey with yellow trim. Mum made our uniforms, which was no mean feat with the yellow featuring

on collars, pockets and cuffs. There was even a belt on the girls' uniform, while the boys' pants were store-bought grey shorts. The girls' hat was the straw kind with elastic to hold it on, although Mum always insisted I keep the elastic in front of my ears and not behind, for fear of ending up looking like a VW with the doors open (not exactly her words).

We called our school bags ports. (The area where students keep their bags at school is still called a port rack, even though most children use backpacks now.) They were a heavy square, composite fibre version of the backpack, with leather straps. Kindy kids had a small carry case. Ours were the Duro brand with a hinged lid and clip at the front, and mine always tended to develop a smell of old bananas. We didn't get a new bag every year — they had to fall apart to warrant the purchase of another. Duro Travel Goods Ltd was registered in 1953 but delisted in 1983. Globite, which began in 1911, was another Australian company that made composite fibre school ports. It is still a leading manufacturer of travel goods.

In the mid 1960s, overhead projectors began their foray into the education scene, revolutionising the way teachers presented their work. While they didn't take over from the blackboard, it was probably the start of many alternative methods. I particularly loved it when our beautiful Grade 4 teacher, Mrs Boulter, would use it. She had blue dyed hair, and when she stood next to the projector, the light would shine through her hair, giving her a halo.

Little pink pots of Perkins Paste were the go-to in class, along with the cone-shaped bottle of white Clag, and the squeezy bottle with the red rubber applicator tip that helped you spread the gum along the paper. These last types often got glued up and you had to peel the dry glue off the top. Perkins Paste had a pretty artistically useless plastic paddle to spread with, but you could flick the glue quite a distance with it (if you were that way inclined). Clag paste's brushes were much more user friendly, although Clag was a wetter medium (made from wheat starch) and could rumple your paper more than Perkins, which was drier and made from a potato dextrin so could technically be eaten (it did happen!). Clag was originally made in the late 1890s and I think, by the consistency and smell, our school still had some of the original bottles. It came in glass bottles with a wooden stick and bristles. These later changed into plastic bottles and plastic bristle brushes. Perkins stopped being produced in the 1980s, but Clag is still a mainstay at school, although the glue stick has been nudging it out.

Much has been written about school milk, so it seems to have been an indelible memory for many, both positive and negative. Federal Parliament decided that providing milk to schoolchildren would be a big help in the nutrition stakes, so passed an Act in 1950 to supply free milk for children under the age of 13. Queensland lagged behind the other states, worrying about the tropical climate and distances between towns, so it started as a trial in Brisbane on 3 March 1953. After it had proven itself, it moved out to the country areas, until eventually over 150,000 Queensland schoolchildren were sipping 30,000 gallons of free milk each week. This was, of course, an enormous boon to the dairy farmers as well. By 1973, a report decided it was poor value for money and the Whitlam government abolished it. The milk came in 1/3 pint (about 175 ml) bottles with straws, but later came in tetra packs where the corners had to be cut off, and in some areas, in plastic bags. Milk monitors were sent from each class to pick up the milk and bring it back to the class. I can't remember it ever being warm or off, as we had it first thing in the morning. I am sure there were kids who hated milk or had a lactose allergy, so unless they had an understanding teacher, it must have been awful for them.

We started to learn to write on a slate. There were lines engraved on one side to help with keeping your writing straight. There was a slate pencil to write with, and a damp sponge, kept in a container, to wipe your slate clean. The sponge was meant to go home each day to be washed out and returned, but there were many times it sat at school overnight (or disgustingly for a whole weekend) to fester. I kept mine in a small yellow box with a clear lid, and Mum would put some disinfectant in with it in the hope that it might slow the bacteria down a bit.

My husband recalls once at the end of the year they were cleaning the slates with some sort of acid, and one of the young female teachers got it on her skirt. The boys stood there gaping as part of her skirt disintegrated, certain that before long she would be walking around the school with nothing on.

I never had to use an inkwell or dip-pen, but the desks still had the holes to hold the bottle. Quink ink was the brand if you were into fountain pens. My father had a fountain pen that he used to keep in his pocket — I still remember the odd occasion when it would leak and the shirt would be stained, usually irretrievably.

While history states that Laszlo Biro invented the first ballpoint pen in 1938 (another was devised in 1888 to mark leather), sales and manufacturers and patent rights swirled around for another 20-odd years. Then along came Baron Bich of France, who dropped the H from his name because, well, it probably sounded like something else, licensed the ballpoint from Biro, and in 1950, started to sell the BIC Cristal pen. You could see through the pen and know how much ink was left, and by the late fifties it had cornered 70 per cent of the European market so that by 2006, 100 billion of them had been sold. In 1954, Parker Pens introduced their version called the Jotter.

I really can't remember using a biro/bic/ballpoint pen much in primary school, relying on my trusty pencils instead. If you did use one and made a mistake, there were the rubbers that were basically half white pencil rubber and half grey ink rubber that had really fine sand mixed into them. They created more of a mess than if you had just crossed out the mistake, leaving gaping holes in your paper from enthusiastic rubbing.

Depending on the level of creativity of your teacher, art would often mean "let's fill in the afternoon session with drawing". The pages were larger than foolscap in size and a buff kind of colour, with one side being super smooth and other a bit rough. We all had colouring-in pencils and would set to work to draw the sun in the top right-hand corner and blue lines across for the sky. If you had an adventurous teacher, you might have indulged in a bright crayon pattern that you then covered in black crayon. Grabbing something sharpish, you would then scratch a picture through the black to have a multi coloured sgraffito imitation. In the meantime, black crayon would have smooshed into the desktop and be all over your hand and anything else you had touched. We loved it!

Art activities were often based on things that were new or just coming onto the market. When I was in around Grade 3, we made things out of the new Styrofoam by cutting shapes with hacksaws and then melting the styrofoam with some sort of heat gun to form an object. Thinking back, there were little bits of the stuff all over the playground, not to mention the noxious fumes we were all sucking in with gay abandon. Would love to do the risk assessment on that activity now!

Copybooks were the bane of my existence. Never known for my beautifully neat handwriting, I hated it and to this day struggle to do running writing, instead developing my own style of running printing. The letters were ridiculously curled and crimped with pot hooks and handles and strokes placed just so. I always felt sorry for the lefties in the class, as inevitably their pages would end up with smudges from moving their hand across what they had just written.

Most children today wouldn't know what a blackboard, is with most of their work either appearing on a digital screen or being written with a texta on a white board. Originally painted with black paint (hence the name), it later changed to green as it supposedly didn't show the dust marks as much. There was a blackboard monitor whose job it was to clean the board in the morning ready for the day's work, and heaven help them if they inadvertently rubbed off something they shouldn't have, like the list of kids who had to do lines. They would also have to take the blackboard dusters outside and bang the dust out of them with a ruler, usually coming back into class covered in chalk dust.

Small used pieces of the Bellco white chalk would be pegged across the room to wake up a pupil who wasn't paying attention. Coloured chalk was always a bit special, and if we were allowed to write on the board, it would be the coloured stuff we grabbed. My teeth still grind when I think of the screech the chalk would make sometimes when pulled across the board.

There was a yard-long blackboard ruler, marked out in inches, with a handle in the middle. It was used for helping to draw lines and angles on the board, and in some classrooms, to bang on the desks to bring back a child's attention. I was fortunate to have never been in a class where the ruler was used on a student, but do know that it happened in other classes in my school.

Cuisenaire rods were developed in the early 1950s by a Belgian primary teacher Georges Cuisenaire as a hands-on learning aid for mathematical exploration, providing a visual way of seeing numbers. Queensland schools embraced the concept, and each child in lower primary had a green plastic box of the different coloured wooden rods. I can always remember the amount of time it took to pack them away systematically so they fitted into the box with the lid on. Although they were a brilliant maths resource, it must have been mind-blowingly frustrating for the teachers.

Much maligned and often remembered with pained expressions, the recorder was the one instrument that all children could play at school as they were cheap and easy to get hold of. Recorder bands were part of many school music programs from the 1930s, and Mt Gravatt was right in the thick of it when I was there. We each had a recorder, mostly plastic by then, and we were meant to clean the accumulated spit after each lesson with a piece of rag threaded through a long plastic needle-like thing. I don't think the rags were ever washed out.

Recorders, when played properly (and good quality), are quite lovely things, but cheaper instruments, coupled with the fact that many teachers didn't really know how to teach the correct "operation", ended up with some of the resulting sounds like cats being strangled.

There was usually a big timber cupboard with doors in the classrooms (especially older buildings) called a press, harking back to older days as the name for a cupboard with shelves in it. They held all sorts of marvels like new books and art equipment. Having a new book with clean white pages was heaven.

The Department of Education supplied books that had a dismally boring grey green cover, with elaborate writing on the front and a cartoon on the back about road safety.

Teachers, or students in higher grades, often had an exercise book with a big deer on the front called The Landseer exercise book.

Mention Dick and Dora, Nip and Fluff to anyone who went to school in the 1950s

and 1960s and they will know who you are talking about. We learned to read with these friends and their stories in the Happy Venture Readers. Written when he was still in England by Professor Fred Schonell of Sir Fred Schonell Drive, St Lucia fame, this reading program was used heavily throughout Australia and the UK, phasing out the Queensland School Readers Prep series in the early 1950s.

These days the class would be stifling giggles every time Dick's name was mentioned. The rest of the Queensland School Readers (or Red Readers as they were fondly known) were eventually replaced in

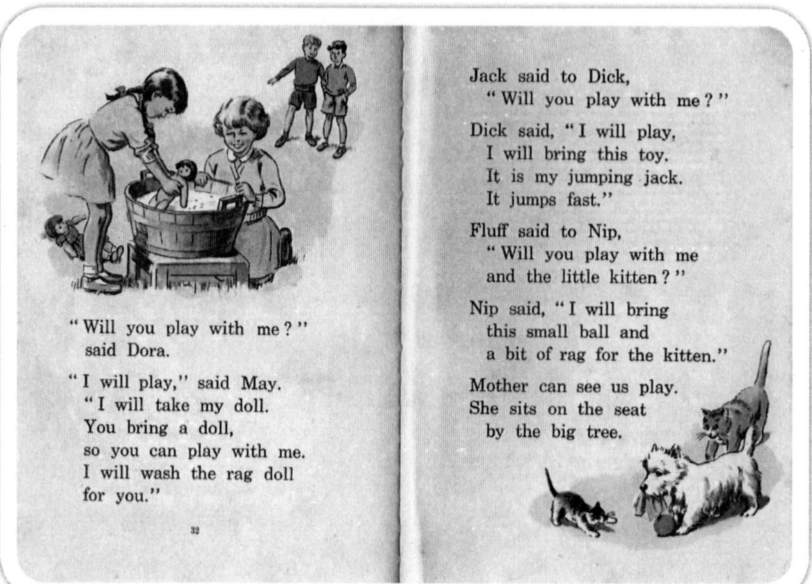

"Will you play with me?"
said Dora.

"I will play," said May.
"I will take my doll.
You bring a doll,
so you can play with me.
I will wash the rag doll
for you."

32

Jack said to Dick,
"Will you play with me?"

Dick said, "I will play,
I will bring this toy.
It is my jumping jack.
It jumps fast."

Fluff said to Nip,
"Will you play with me
and the little kitten?"

Nip said, "I will bring
this small ball and
a bit of rag for the kitten."

Mother can see us play.
She sits on the seat
by the big tree.

the late 1960s, but not until they had scarred countless young lives with their literary version of *The Little Match Girl.*

The cards from the SRA Reading Laboratory provided a multi-level literacy comprehension activity that must have been a godsend to teachers for those kids that finished their work early. "Go and do an SRA card." They had all sorts of different subjects and topics, and yes, I was one of those nerdy kids that actually liked doing them.

School banking began in 1931 and operated through the Commonwealth Savings Bank which, before privatisation, was the government-owned bank. My father, who was the deputy at Upper Mt Gravatt State School, occasionally brought home a few Commonwealth Bank pencils. There was nothing better than having a brand new pencil, especially as they were gold and silver. However, so that I learned responsible consumerism, I had to pay Dad two cents if I wanted one. The Commonwealth Bank also had a metal money box in the shape of a big Commonwealth Bank building.

Long before stickers were the essence of bribery at school (I mean, "reward"), teachers had rubber stamps that could range from "Excellent work" with a rabbit to "Try harder next time" with a monkey, which kind of negated the issue really because you still got a stamp (or made you feel like the proverbial because you HAD tried)!!!

ABC began its television broadcasts for schools in 1962, although at that stage not many schools had televisions. When they did get them, they might have had one or two, perhaps in the library or Grade 7 rooms, and classes would be taken to see whatever the program was. When the moon landing happened in 1969, any child who had a television set at home was allowed to go home so they could watch the live action. I wandered home and sat with my Barbie dolls watching Neil do his thing. My brother, who was in Grade 7 at the time, stayed at school and his class was shepherded in next door where there was one of the school TVs.

Large grey speakers in the corners of the room were there for the principal to make school announcements, to play the national anthem each morning and "All Things Bright and Beautiful", or something similarly religious, for us to sing to. ABC also had radio programs for schools that were played over these speakers.

I guess as a bit of an attempt to curb the spread of germs, every child was expected to have a hanky each day at school. In Grade 2, at our morning assemblies, the call went out for those who did not have a hanky to stand up. Complete humiliation then flooded the room as everyone sang the "Piggy Sniffles" song. Our wonderful teacher, Mrs McAllister, had a supply of Kleenex (which was awesome in itself) and would make sure that everyone was covered.

Sniffles was the name of a clever little pig

He could play the violin he could do the Irish jig

But the other little piggies wouldn't ask him out to tea

'Cos he never had a handkerchief, no not he

He never had a handkerchief, no not he

The poor kids who were standing were squirming with embarrassment. Some mums insisted on pinning the hankies onto the fronts of the uniforms, where they looked OK in the morning, but after a day of sniffles, weren't so beguiling.

I do remember seeing children whose legs were held in iron calipers as a result of contracting polio. By 1953, Australia had 10,000 people (including children) per year being hit with polio. A couple of years later, the polio vaccine had been developed, and by the end of the 1950s, thankfully, the disease had been all but eradicated. We had our vaccine at school which was, by then, the Sabin oral vaccine, and was a tasty pink pearl drop of liquid on a spoon. We also had the multi-pronged vaccination for smallpox. My forward-thinking Mum insisted on having mine on the inside of my forearm so I did not end up with a scar on my shoulder. I am forever grateful for the government providing vaccinations to all children to prevent these two incredibly devastating diseases.

Play equipment of the day would not come close to meeting stringent standards now, but we LOVED it. The Jungle Gym was basically a cube of cross bars and uprights that we climbed and swung through. The swings and see-saws knocked out a few teeth and split a few chins, and the metal slippery slides burnt your backside on really hot days.

Of course, grass was sometimes sparse and allowed to grow a little longer than it is on today's carefully maintained ovals. We had to be awake to those vindictive types who would tie the long pieces of grass together and make grass traps to catch the unwary as they ran across the oval.

We learned our own version of risk management through trial and error, and fortunately for me, apart from a broken arm sliding down a banister rail, I survived intact. Oh, there was that one time in kindy where I got hit on the head with a big piece of conglomerate by a girl who thought I was playing with my bucket and spade a bit too close to her boyfriend, but I didn't see that one coming.

Before plastic packaging took hold of the school lunch boxes, our school had two kinds of rubbish bins in the lunch area. One was painted red and it was for paper bags, greaseproof paper from sandwiches, paddle pop sticks (though we often collected these) or other non-food items. This was hauled off to the concrete incinerator at the back of the school and burnt. The other bin was painted green and was for food scraps like banana skins, apple cores or bread leftovers. There probably wasn't a huge amount each day as most kids would eat all their lunch, never tossing away a good sandwich. These scraps were picked up by the pig man to feed his animals.

The toilets were the old gravity flush pull chain ones, with the cistern sitting up high on the wall. They were always dank and dark, and you only went if you really, really, absolutely had to. Sometimes you might be lucky (??) to find a cracked, faded piece of Sunlight soap lurking in the basin. If you walked blindfolded around the school, you could always smell where the boys' toilets were situated (actually, you still can these days, especially the junior ones!).

I cannot finish up until I mention the greaseproof paper on a roll that was meant to be toilet paper. I don't know how it was meant to "absorb" anything as it was super smooth and shiny, and must have blocked the pipes.

The unsealed sealed section

Stuff that either ... (a) we weren't supposed to know about or (b) nobody talked about

Naughty magazines had been around for a while, but became more risqué the further into the 1960s you progressed. Australia had had *Man* magazine (and its offshoots) since the 1930s with its painted pictures of scantily clad women. However, during the 1950s, American girlie magazines like *Playboy*, which launched in 1953, descended on the Australian market at much cheaper prices. Moving into the 1960s, these magazines were reducing the clothing content considerably, and censorial Queensland was having paroxysms, struggling to hold back the tide at the border.

Australasian Post ("the mag with the most"), available in all good barbershops, provided a legitimate goggle at bikini-clad cover girls, while *Pix* magazine was another barbershop library edition with photo competitions for the next pin-up girl. *People* magazine had, yes, more bikini girls and sex stories to titillate. These were all quite tame in comparison to what was coming in from America (which is interesting considering their reaction to nudity on television or at the beach).

The trip to the mechanics with dad to get the car serviced was always an interesting one as we craned our necks over the counter to check out the dubious calendars they had hanging on the wall of the workroom. Pin-up girls in various poses and amounts of clothing (usually not very much) smiled out from the depths of the darkness and grime, ostensibly to remind the mechanics just what day it was and when Mrs Henry's car should be finished. These were a far cry from the calendar we had on the back of our dunny with a picture of a boy and his dog hiding behind the kennel, while his father called him to help with the mowing.

Many of the pin-up girls were paintings (and apparently didn't look a whole like the original model), with photographic calendars not appearing until much later. The calendars were usually linked to some supplier like Champion, Pirelli, NGK or Bridgestone, and had little tear off months right at the bottom so as not to risk damaging the pert image when you tore July off.

On the flip side were the men's magazines aimed at the he-man in every male, with blood, gore and animals with big teeth. There were stories of war, the Wild West, survival, crime ... and animals with big teeth just waiting to rip the flesh off your muscly, sweaty arms. These were available at your friendly barbershop too, and were immensely popular in the late 1950s, gradually fading out as *Playboy* and *Hustler* replaced them with a different kind of sweat.

Not so much a thing in the southern suburbs of Brisbane (I don't think anyway ...), but there is the old connection with the box of Omo in the window and wives behaving badly. Connotations of the acronym are "Old Man Out", "Old Man Overseas" or "On My Own".

The concept of condoms has been around for centuries, but latex condoms were invented in 1919. It was thinner than rubber and didn't smell ... rubbery. The 1950s saw improvements with a reservoir tip, and thinner, lighter and tighter latex. Lubricant was added as well. The Ansell Rubber Company was founded in Australia in 1929 by Eric Ansell. Eric began developing condoms, and then other latex products like disposable gloves. Ansell's Checker Threes (now called Chekmate) condoms have been slipped into back pockets for decades in

Australia, although it wasn't always easy for the young buck about town.

There were restrictions on contraceptive advertising or sale displays, and it was secret business to buy them at the chemist, hoping like hell that the girl shop assistant was busy stocking shelves. On the pack they were called prophylactic — to prevent disease from happening. Really, just disease????

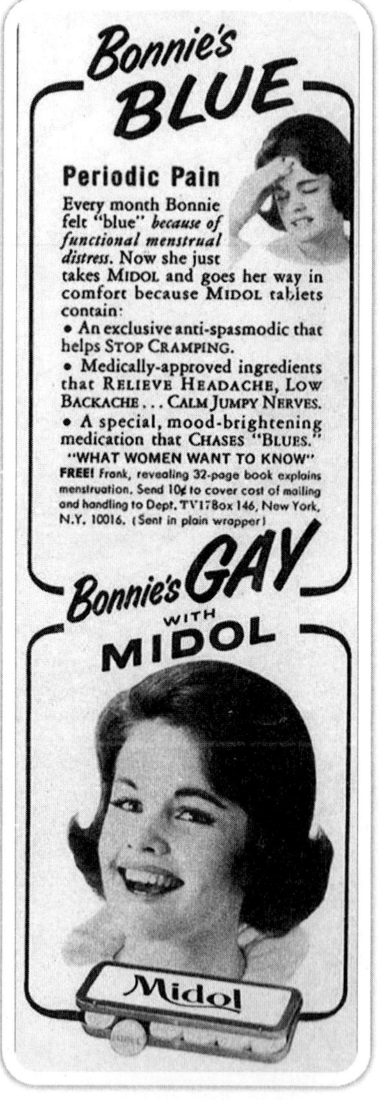

Women's periods were certainly not part of general, polite conversation, even though they were a huge part of their lives for multiple reasons. Aside from the inconvenience of those few days each month, there were lots of other factors at play. Period pain was just accepted as the norm, and women struggled through the best they could. Painkillers of the time like Aspro, Bex and Vincents would not touch some of the pain that many women experienced.

Sanitary items have come a long way in the last 50 years, thank goodness. Prior to the disposable items, women had pieces of fabric that they folded and then attached to what was tastefully called a menstrual belt, or pinned them to their underwear with safety pins. These "rags" were washed and re-used multiple times. Of course, there was no such thing as waterproof linings, so accidents did occur.

The disposable napkin had been around in the States for a long time, with Modess, in 1928, even issuing what they called "silent purchasing coupons" so you wouldn't have to mention your period. In fact, wealthy Australians had been able to purchase disposable pads by the late 1920s, but it wasn't really till after the Second World War that things began to change for the average woman.

By the 1960s, most women were using some form of disposable pad, still attaching them to a menstrual belt, but at least they didn't have to wash them out. Modess (a Johnson & Johnson company) vied for market share with Kotex (part of Kimberley-Clark). The pads were so big and cumbersome that they were "fondly" known as surfboards, and felt like you had a continual wedgie. In 1969 Stayfree (also part of Johnson & Johnson) added an adhesive strip — a liberating

golden moment when women got to throw their menstrual belt in the trash.

Tampons (the modern version at least) were invented in 1931 (by a man mind you), but were originally sold only to married women, while younger women were discouraged from using them as they were thought to be sexually improper. Tampons gradually increased market share during the 1960s, partly due to the advertising focusing on the physical freedom they gave you. Still, many old schoolers wouldn't go near them and stuck to their surfboards.

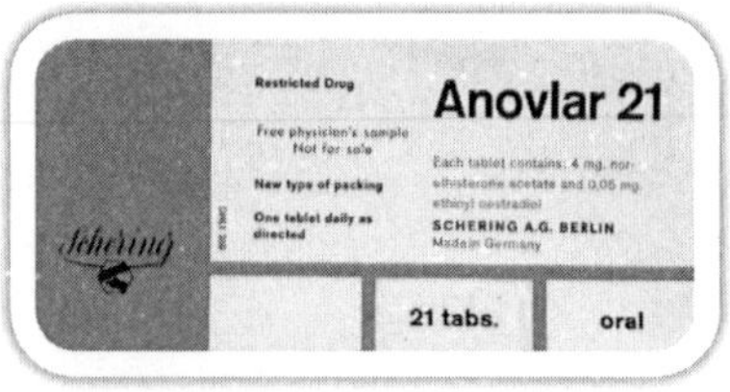

In 1961, the Pill was released in Australia, the second country in the world to make it available. Called Anovlar, it was only available to married women and then only on prescription. And to add insult to injury, a 27.5 per cent luxury tax was slugged on top of it, which wasn't removed until 1972 when it was placed on PBS. The advent of the Pill gave women more of a choice with their family planning, and subsequently led to a significant increase by 1964 of females entering the workforce. Contraceptive use in Australia was less than 30 per cent in the 1950s. This jumped to over 90 per cent 40 years later. It was not something you talked about with the girls though.

Hailed in the 1960s as the new wonder drug, Valium sidled its way into many bathroom cabinets becoming the "Mother's little helper" in a Rolling Stones song from 1967. Developed as the quick fix for grief, stress, depression and anxiety, a couple of sceptical Roche executives tried it out on their mothers-in-law and were pleasantly surprised by the calming results. It went on to sell billions.

Vibrators were first developed as a medical aid to relieve tension, but with human ingenuity, they were sometimes turned to other matters. Original ones were plugged into the wall or were hand cranked, bit like a rotary beater. Given the fact that the burgeoning adult movie scene in the 1920s was portraying them in a different light, the advertising slowed down and they weren't mentioned in polite society.

Massagers, legitimately used in various situations such as a head massager used by the barber, were creatively used for other, some would say greater, purposes. Settings were introduced to either speed up or slow down the movements.

The development of portable batteries and their ever-decreasing size, portability (and safety) and size (and shape) led many to a rethink in design. Repurposed massagers of the 1960s, now included vibrating cushions, were made for both internal and external "medical" uses. The sexual revolution of the 1960s led to version two of "Mother's little helper", and by the late 1960s, Hitachi had launched its Magic Wand, which still sells extremely well.

Scanty Panties (affectionately known as Scanties) were open-leg underwear such as French knickers or tap pants, as opposed to elasticised leg bands (which were called briefs). They were made from fabric such as Milanese that was soft and light. There was a saying about scanties during the war when the American soldiers were in town — "One yank and they're down".

Prior to Don Chipp's reign as Customs Minister in 1969, federal censorship of literature was a contentious issue, with no real guidelines for what was appropriate or inappropriate. Customs officials made a decision and referred it to a panel of "experts" to make a judgement, with offensive obscenity being the main reason for banning a book, and a few banned for sedition or blasphemy.

Many banned titles are quite familiar today, including *Lady Chatterley's Lover* (banned from 1928 to 1965), *Lolita* (banned from 1958 to 1965), *Peyton Place* (original edition banned from 1957 to 1971 although there was an Australian edition with certain scenes removed), *Another Country* by James Baldwin, which contained inter-racial sex (banned from 1962 to 1966), and *The Naked Lunch* by William Burroughs, with its homosexual and drug-related content (banned from 1959 to 1973 and called the "crudest book" — one of the last works to remain on the prohibited list).

Even poor old Norman Lindsay was not spared with his titles *Red Heap* (banned from 1930 to 1958) and *Cautious Amorist* (banned from 1933 to 1953). The list is long, with titles we take for granted on the library shelf — *Lord of the Flies, Fahrenheit 451, Catcher in the Rye, The Spy Who Loved Me, The Lily and the Pillar* and, dare I mention it, *The Kama Sutra.*

It was not only books that were forbidden. There were popular and pulp fiction titles with lurid covers like *Road Floozie* and *Love Me Sailor*, or *True Crime* and *Best Detective Cases. Love Illustrated*, a romance comic, was banned in Queensland in 1954. I can't imagine what scenes of anguish and blood-letting there would have been if *Shades of Grey* had been released in 1954.

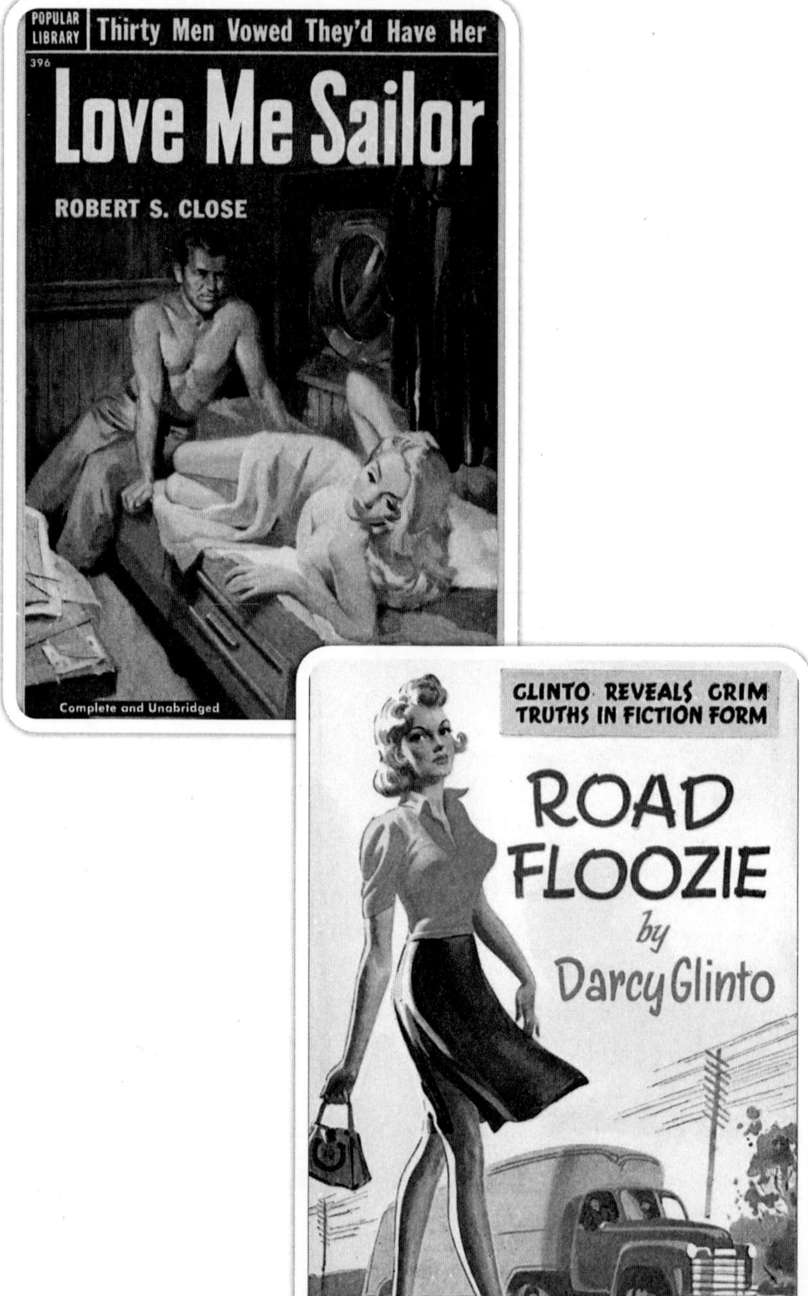
POPULAR LIBRARY
Thirty Men Vowed They'd Have Her
396
Love Me Sailor
ROBERT S. CLOSE
Complete and Unabridged
GLINTO REVEALS GRIM TRUTHS IN FICTION FORM
ROAD FLOOZIE
by
Darcy Glinto
SIX SHILLINGS NET

Some of my own stuff (stuff my mates told me) ...

Some of my own stuff (stuff my mates told me) ...

Recipe stuff

Carnation Milk Ice Cream

1 level teaspoon gelatine

2 tablespoons water

1 level tablespoon butter

3 rounded tablespoons castor sugar

1 teaspoon vanilla essence

375 ml can Carnation evaporated milk chilled

Pinch of salt

1 tablespoon lemon juice

Place gelatine and water in a saucepan and allow to stand for two to three minutes. Stir over a low heat until dissolved. Add the butter and allow to melt. Stir in the sugar and vanilla. Cool. Beat the chilled Carnation Milk in a chilled bowl with a pinch of salt and tablespoon of lemon juice until stiff. Gradually add the cooled gelatin mixture, beating continually. Pour into trays and freeze.

Honey Milk Velvet

Dissolve 2 teaspoons of gelatine in ¼ cup of hot water. Add 1½ tablespoons of honey and stir slowly into ½ pint of milk. Bring ¼ pint of milk to the boil and stir in mixture. Add vanilla and 1 junket tablet crushed and dissolved in a little water. Set in fridge.

Steamed Pudding

Mix 1 tablespoon of margarine with 1 cup self-raising flour and add 1 cup of chopped dates. Mix to a stiff cake mix with milk and put in an ungreased basin.

Mix 1 tablespoon of honey, ½ cup sugar, 2 dessertspoons margarine, 1 tablespoon of coconut and ½ cup boiling water. Pour it over the cake mix and stand in uncovered

saucepan of boiling water halfway up the side for ½ hour.

Vanilla Slice with SAOs

Cover the base of an oven tray with a layer of SAO biscuits, if necessary, cut to fit. Make a thick vanilla custard, almost to blanc mange consistency. Pour immediately over SAO biscuit base to approximately ¾" thickness. Quickly cover with another layer of SAO biscuits before skin can form on the custard. Make a thin passionfruit or vanilla icing and spread over top layer of SAOs. Set aside to cool and, when firm, cut into squares. Serve plain or with cream.

Referencey stuff

While much of this is the ramblings of a 50-something's brain, along with the thoughts of friends and family, websites were visited to gain background and historical information. Those referenced below were used, along with the websites belonging to specific brands.

www.Adelaidenow.com.au

www.artofmanliness.com/articles/vintage-mens-adventure-magazines/

www.asaleocare.com/news/celebrating-65-years-of-sorbent/

www.ashet.org.au/wp-content/uploads/2015/09/News-July-14.pdf

www.australiangeographic.com.au/topics/history-culture/2017/07/timeline-a-short-history-of-australian-tea/

www.letslookagain.com/tag/peek-frean-history/

www.australianweaving.com.au/about-us/

www.australianmuseum.net.au

www.bestride.com/news/entertainment/your-first-car-the-history-of-matchbox-toys

www.blancoandbull.com/boot-cleaning/boot-care-history/

www.blog.naa.gov.au/banned/

www.blogs.slq.qld.gov.au/jol/tag/banned-books/

www.britannica.com/topic/Milanese-knit-textile

www.ccsretro.com/internet-myth-nally-gay-ware/

www.coca-colajourney.com.au

www.collection.maas.museum/object/399975

www.collections.museumvictoria.com.au/items/1712859

www.csiropedia.csiro.au/softly-detergent/

www.Discovermagazine.com.au

www.dwell.com/collection/britains-mid-century-female-designers (many of the fabric design samples on the memory pages)

www.education.qld.gov.au/about-us/history/history-topics/queensland-school-readers

www.emelbourne.net.au/biogs/EM01127b.htm

www.flickrhivemind.net/Tags/nightsoil/Timeline

www.formica.com/en-us/about-us

www.Gracesguide.co.uk

www.Judithsalecich.com

www.mathmos.com.au

www.mentalfloss.com/article/92787/8-vintage-hairstyling-products-your-grandmother-probably-swore

www.milo.com.au/all-about-milo/history

www.mortein.com.au/about/about-mortein

www.ncbi.nlm.nih.gov/pubmed/14696703

www.news.com.au/feature/special-features/the-rich-history-of-australias-favourite-canned-soup/news-story/e8d7cdb7836d92317f4a2db22361b26b

www.news.com.au/finance/business/media/drug-addict-prostitute-destitute-and-dead-tragic-end-for-the-rinso-kids-advertisings-ideal-family/news-story/0d6ea77e0f5bd0b318d229f0cde16b18

www.nfsa.gov.au/latest/radio-and-tv-licences

www.paulineconolly.com/2017/dolly-pegs-by-the-derwent/dolly pegs/factory

www.quora.com/How-do-you-buy-condoms-Dont-you-get-shy

www.redheads.com.au/history-milestones/

www.smh.com.au/lifestyle/coffee-by-numbers-20060718-gdnzbj.html

www.startsat60.com/discover/entertainment/jokes/do-you-remember-the-sound-of-the-ice-cream-van

www.surplusvalue.org.au/McQueen/p_war_aus/Eco/pwar_aus_ec_softdrinks.htm

www.televisionau.com/feature-articles/tv-week

www.theage.com.au/national/accidental-addicts-20030616-gdvvx8.html

www.theconversation.com/the-ongoing-taboo-of-menstruation-in-australia-53984

www.thoughtco.com/ballpoint-pens-laszlo-biro-4078959

Chapman, R 2002, *Aniseed Balls, Billy Carts and Clotheslines An ABC of Growing up in the Thirties*, Pamela Van der Kooy, Brisbane.

Slade GD, Spencer, AJ, Davies MJ & Stewart JF 1996, "Caries experience among children in fluoridated Townsville and unfluoridated Brisbane", *Australian and New Zealand Journal of Public Health*, 20:623–9.